# KILLER COUPLES

TAMMY COHEN

# KILLER COUPLES

## TRUE STORIES OF PARTNERS IN CRIME

JB
JOHN BLAKE

Published by John Blake Publishing Ltd,
3 Bramber Court, 2 Bramber Road,
London W14 9PB, England

www.blake.co.uk

First published in paperback in 2008

ISBN 978 1 84454 572 8



British Library Cataloguing-in-Publication Data:

A catalogue record for this book is available from the British Library.

Design by www.envydesign.co.uk

Printed and bound in Great Britain by CPD Group, Blaina, Abertillery, Wales

1 3 5 7 9 10 8 6 4 2



Papers used by John Blake Publishing are natural, recyclable products made from wood grown in sustainable forests. The manufacturing processes conform to the environmental regulations of the country of origin.

Every attempt has been made to contact the relevant copyright-holders, but some were unobtainable. We would be grateful if the appropriate people could contact us.

# CONTENTS

# PREFACE

Before you read any further, be warned. The stories in this book will leave you appalled and traumatised; worse still, they will shake your faith in human nature. Certainly that's how it was for me as I researched each gruesome case with growing horror. When writing about lone killers, at least there's the consolation of telling oneself that this was one isolated, deluded individual. Writing about couples who kill removes even that crumb of comfort.

These are disturbing cases that will make you question everything you know, or *think* you know, about who we are and what we are capable of. Our immediate instinct is to classify the perpetrators as monsters, alien creatures that exist outside our comprehension and yet if that's the case, how is it that such exotic creatures manage to find one another? How many of them must there be to be able to pair off with such sickening regularity? Of course, the truth is that there are no monsters, only monstrous crimes that grow out of a particular dynamic between two people. That dynamic is what I have tried to focus on in telling these terrible stories. As far as can be ascertained, all the facts are accurate, but, inevitably, some small liberties have been taken in bringing people and events to life to understand them better.

In 1997, in a letter to the then home secretary, Ian Brady referred to the child murders he committed with Myra Hindley as 'marriage ceremonies theoretically binding us ever closer'. While the Moors Murders have been analysed so many times as to make their retelling in this book unnecessary, Brady's words offer a chilling insight into this most warped and most dangerous dynamic. The couple that kills together stays together – bound by their secrets, their knowledge of one another, and by the blood rituals they've shared.

Writing these stories wasn't easy, but it was grimly fascinating in terms of what it revealed about the secret underbelly of human relationships. I hope reading them provides the same experience. Just make sure you leave the light on!

Tammy Cohen

# INTRODUCTION

A 14-year-old girl is kept for days as a sex slave, filmed begging for her life and then strangled. Two 8-year-olds are snatched off the street and left to starve in an underground dungeon. A man's head is staved in with a hammer before he's stabbed 66 times, his blood collected in a bowl to be drunk. A vulnerable man is held prisoner in a garden shed, then tortured to death... Sadly, there is nothing unique about violent death. Since records began there have been no shortage of accounts bearing witness to man's tremendous capacity for inhumanity. But what makes the above crimes so shocking is that they are not the work of one depraved individual but a couple acting together. In a world where brutality has become so commonplace that we are almost immune to it, the juxtaposition of love and savagery, of romance and sadism, can still make us sit up and take notice.

We Westerners hold very little sacred, but one of our last, most fiercely protected ideals is that of the redemptive power of love. With the right person by our side, we insist, individuals who were once broken can be healed, lives that were going off track can be set straight again... The love that inspires sonnets, poetry and even Whitney Houston ballads is what we're all searching for because it represents the key to another kingdom, where past wrongs are put right and shattered hearts become whole. Love lifts us up where we belong, we're told. And where we belong is this better place – beyond loneliness, isolation and acts of desperation borne of bitterness and despair. Put simply, love – at least the kind of love we choose to believe in – is a power for good.

So pervasive is this view, so seductive the premise, that when something happens to cast doubt over it, we cannot, simply will not, believe it. Lovers should be heroes, not psychopaths; they should be kissing rather than killing. Their prize should be mutual salvation, not contamination.

The romantic comedies we flock to see, the love songs we sing along to, all share one clear message: love makes you a better person. Which is why crimes such as the ones described above send such shockwaves through us all. Here are couples lucky enough to find love, which is after all, our modern-day holy grail. But instead of redemption, they institute rape; instead of salvation, sadism; and instead of devotion, death.

Individually, they may have been broken from the start, but rather than fixing them, love shatters them still further into millions of irreparable pieces. This is not the noble, true love we know from a thousand big-screen love stories, but love that exalts in power, that feeds on misery, that wallows in violence. This is a love that's twisted and warped out of all recognition – and yet it is still love.

The couples featured in this book are not inspired to be better people because they found each other. Instead they're encouraged to be worse. Rather than boosting one another's strengths, they exploit each other's weaknesses. You would think you might be able to spot them, wouldn't you, these freaks of nature who turn romance into a blood sport? And that's another reason why they so disturb us: their very normality. They kidnap, they rape, they murder, torture and abuse… And in between they make each other cups of tea, run baths, buy birthday gifts, have sex and tour their local DIY store together on rainy bank holidays. Love may have created a monster, but it's a monster that wears a scarily ordinary face.

Pretty, petite blonde-haired Karla Homolka and her handsome young fiancé cooked her parents a Father's Day meal, while the dead body of the young girl they'd just assaulted lay festering among the bags of potatoes in their cellar. Rose West broke off from the most violent sexual abuse to make her husband and their victim a cup of tea. Kenny Kimes stopped off at a florist's on his way home from disposing of the body of the man he'd just murdered to buy the woman he loved a bunch of flowers…

It's not the differences between these couples and any other couple in love that makes them so terrifying; it's the similarities. You wouldn't spot them if you saw them walking towards you, hand in hand. If they moved in next door, you wouldn't know them. It's our ability to recognise love, but not evil.

Of course, not all killer couples are cut from the same cloth. There's not one neat template defining them all. Some couples in this book would probably not have killed if they hadn't met. Something in the way they reacted with each other, in the timing of their coming together, created the soil in which the germ of violence was allowed to grow. Would Ann Hunter and Anton Lee, two well-respected professionals, have solicited for murder if they hadn't happened to have met each other and had those first drunken conversations, which spiralled out of control? Would the two couples who imprisoned and tortured vulnerable young men have graduated from bullying to murder if fate hadn't thrown them into each other's paths?

In other cases, there's a high probability that one of the partnership, usually the woman, would probably have gone on to lead a largely uneventful life, if they had not been sucked into the malevolent orbit of a psychopathic partner. Michelle Martin, wife of Marc Dutroux, the Beast of Belgium, was remarkable only for her unremarkableness, for her lack of moral weight, her lack of substance... Would she have gone on to commit the atrocities of which she was found guilty had she never crossed paths with her perverted husband? Rebecca Harris had a mean temper and a sharp tongue, but would she have stabbed anyone, if not for the influence of murderous lover

Stephen Marsh? Would Kenneth Kimes now be facing a future behind bars if he'd never come into the clutches of the materialist, domineering Sante?

Then there are the other couples, the ones whose proclivity towards what is most base and most vile, what degrades and what destroys is the very thing that first brings them together. What most attracts each to the other is the image of their own worst selves reflected back at them. Rose and Fred West each killed individually, but in each other they found a soul mate in savagery, someone whose sexual sadism and lust for power mirrored their own, and, by mirroring it, made it seem normal, acceptable, even desirable.

Whatever their particular make up, in the end couples that kill affront everything we hold most dear. We want to be able to pigeonhole our psychopaths in order to recognise them when we find them: loners in bed-sits who can't form normal relationships, misfits and freaks. We don't want them to be the couple next door, the newlyweds across the street. Most of all, we don't want them to be truly in love.

As a society, we pride ourselves on being realistic, cynical even. And yet the need to believe that love conquers all permeates every aspect of our lives. Love is good, we tell our children: love is the answer. The couples in this book have known great love, but in the end, it's that very love that corrupts and maims, that rapes and slaughters. In that, they become our worst nightmare.

CHAPTER 1

# THE FIRST CUT IS THE DEEPEST

STEPHEN MARSH AND REBECCA HARRIS

Red marks were appearing on her inner wrists where the cord tying her to the bedposts rubbed against her pale, exposed skin, but Rebecca Harris hardly noticed. Besides, with the blindfold obscuring her vision, she couldn't see anything anyway.

Lying in the darkness, Rebecca felt her whole body tense. The anticipation was unbearable.

'Here it comes. You know you like it.' The voice was hoarse, teasing.

Rebecca took a deep breath, her ribcage rising sharply under the tight, black corset. And then she felt it. Sharp and cold against her goose-pimpled flesh, the blade of the knife was stroking her thigh, gently at first and then with increasing pressure. Her breath escaped in a low moan of excitement mixed with something else: fear.

'You love that, don't you?' Now he was running the blade along her arm and she could feel a trickle of blood running down towards her elbow. Then another sensation: soft, moist. His tongue was languorously licking it up.

'We could be together all the time like this, if you'd just do as I ask,' his voice, with its gentle South Wales accent, was gentle, but insistent.

'I'd do anything for you, you know that,' her words came out in a high-pitched rush, and she hated the note of desperation in her voice. Of course, he picked up on that right away.

'So why won't you do this one thing?' he was wheedling now. 'We could be together forever. Wouldn't you like that?'

Of course she would. Ever since she'd started her affair with Stephen Marsh eight months before, Rebecca Harris had wanted nothing else but to spend every moment with him. She'd done whatever he'd asked her, even going along with the cutting, the bondage, the whips… enjoying it for his sake because this was what he wanted. But this was something else. And yet, if she didn't do it, he might leave her. He'd had other lovers before her, and she knew he'd have no problem finding someone else to replace her. He was so good-looking, so charismatic… She didn't know what she'd do without him.

As if he was reading her thoughts, he stepped up the pressure.

'I love you, you know that. I just want us to be together all the time, the way we're meant to be.'

He was saying all the right things, all the things she longed to hear.

'And we could be – if only you'd do this one thing for me. If only you'd kill my wife…'

Of course he was married. The good-looking ones always were, Rebecca thought, eyeing up Stephen Marsh at the Swansea Directory Enquiries call centre where the pair were working. Youthful-looking for his 36 years, with dark hair and blue eyes that, when he fixed them on you, made you feel as if you were the only person that mattered… All the women had a soft spot for Stephen. Anyway, rumour had it that he took his marriage vows with a large pinch of salt, enjoying a series of girlfriends on the side.

Well, good on him! That's what Rebecca thought. Married herself for nearly five years to a man forty years her senior, she had had plenty of time to dwell on the drawbacks of monogamy. Looking back on it, she couldn't imagine what had possessed her to agree to marry Ronald Harris, who'd been 65 when they walked down the aisle. With the bride just 25, he'd been old enough to be her grandfather.

Of course, the security had been a big factor, particularly once she'd got pregnant with their 5-year-old son – Ron had been a reasonably successful businessman and the couple led a comfortable life. But the age gap was always going to be a problem, and as the marriage went on, Rebecca found herself more and more resentful of her OAP husband and flying into increasingly violent rages. Their frequent rows were bitter and full of venom and vitriol; she was left shaking with anger.

No, marriage was not an institution Rebecca Harris held in high regard.

'You're gorgeous, do you know that?' Stephen Marsh's twinkling blue eyes locked onto hers and, to her annoyance, she could feel herself blushing.

'Fancy coming for a drink with me after work?'

Rebecca could hardly bring herself to meet his gaze. She'd heard the expression 'undressing you with his eyes' before, but she'd never actually known what that meant. At least until now.

'I'm married,' she muttered, the fingers of her right hand furiously twisting the wedding ring she'd come to despise.

'That's all right,' he grinned. 'So am I!'

Over that night and the weeks and months that followed, Rebecca got to know all about Stephen Marsh. She knew he'd been married for 13 years to a Sikh woman called Jaspal that he'd met while working for the Ministry of Defence in London. Jaspal's strictly religious family had never approved of him, he'd told her. Neither had they liked the fact that the couple left the MoD to run pubs. That's why they'd ended up coming back to Swansea, Stephen's home town.

Of course, when he was telling this story to Rebecca, Stephen left out the part about Jaspal being fed up with him flirting with all the female customers and the girls working behind the bar. And how being around alcohol all the time caused his drinking, always prodigious, to get completely out of control. But then, as Rebecca would learn for herself, Stephen Marsh was very proficient at manipulating the truth when it suited him.

At first when they'd made love, Stephen had been a caring and affectionate lover. Invariably it had happened at the smart house he shared with Jaspal on an executive housing estate in Gorseinon, West Swansea, on the site of an old colliery. Understandably, Rebecca had been nervous at the beginning. Even though Jaspal had a demanding job at an insurance company in the city centre which kept her out of the house for long hours, the place still bore another woman's stamp. When the Marsh's old dog, Bwbach, gazed up at her, Rebecca couldn't help detecting a touch of reproach in her big brown eyes. No wonder she had found it hard to relax, jumping every time she heard a car door slam outside. But Stephen was so sexy and so full of confidence that nothing would go wrong that Rebecca soon lost her initial nerves and began to enjoy their sessions.

It felt so good to have a younger lover again, someone whose lithe, taut body and sexual stamina more than matched her own. She loved looking at him naked, devouring him with her eyes so that she could recreate every detail in her fantasies when she was once again back home with Ron.

But rapidly, Stephen's sexual demands began to change. He became rougher in bed, less focused on her and more on his own pleasure. He started calling her a whore and asking her to dress up in fetishistic clothing. Sometimes he'd even slap her about. But then in the next breath, he'd be so loving, so tender that Rebecca would feel as if her insides were melting. Anyway, by that stage, she was in love and determined to do everything she could to keep her man and make him happy.

So she bought a whole selection of black fetishist-style underwear, which she'd cram into a bag and bring into work on the days when she knew she was meeting up with Stephen. And she repeated back the words he wanted to hear. 'I'm a whore,' she'd groan, knowing how it turned him on.

At first, though, when he'd brought up the subject of using a knife during sex, she refused to listen.

'You want me to do *what*?' she'd shrieked, unable to believe what she'd just heard.

'I want you to cut me. Just a little bit,' he'd repeated. 'Then you lick up the blood. Don't worry, it's nice,' he'd assured her, seeing her disgusted expression. 'It's a real turn-on, you'll see.'

'No way!' had been her initial response. But, as with so many things, when he'd persevered enough, she'd eventually given in. There was just something about Stephen that made women want to do what he said, even when it went against everything they'd previously thought about themselves. He was that kind of guy.

To her surprise, Rebecca found herself not only using the knife on Stephen, but letting him do it to her as well. The first time she'd been terrified, and then angry. He'd promised only to cut her once, but then he'd launched into a kind of frenzy, slicing the blade across her skin, again and again.

'I'm not doing that again!' she fumed. But of course she had – she never could deny him anything for long. And he was right. It *was* a turn-on. Well, it was a turn-on for her to see how turned-on he was getting! Bizarrely, considering she was trussed up and it was her own blood that was trickling down her thighs, it gave her a feeling of power to witness his mounting excitement and to know that it was all because of her. It was just more proof, she decided, of how much they loved each other. If only they could be together all the time; if only they didn't both have to go home to other people at the end of the day, she thought.

'We could always bump them off,' joked Stephen, after another discussion about their respective spouses and how wonderful it would be if they didn't exist. But when he started to bring the subject up again and again, Rebecca began to wonder whether he really was joking after all. Sometimes it was so hard to tell with Stephen.

'We'll kill Ron,' he'd tell her, enthusiastically outlining some plan for doing away with her ageing husband. 'Then I'll divorce Jaz and we'll be together.'

But the next time she saw him he'd have changed his mind about getting divorced. Why should he give up his flash home and yuppy lifestyle? No, they'd kill Jaspal instead.

Rebecca's answer was always the same. 'Stop messing about, Steve,' she'd say, annoyed that he was wasting the precious time they had together with more of his ridiculous plans. But increasingly, Stephen wouldn't be put off.

'I thought you loved me,' he'd snap at her, his eyes suddenly cold and devoid of any affection.

'I do,' Rebecca would stammer, desperate to see the tenderness return to his now-icy gaze.

In the pub after work, or in the car driving home, the conversation would inevitably turn back towards the same subject. Now he'd dropped the talk of killing Ron and his focus was entirely on Jaspal – and how good life could be if she was out of the picture.

'I just want us to be together,' Stephen would say, giving her the full force of that 'special' look that made her forget about everything else in the world.

Things became so intense that Rebecca would almost dread being alone with him, although, paradoxically, this was also what she most craved. Their embraces were still passionate, burning with the heat of the emotions both were having to suppress at home, but now there was an undercurrent of tension that hadn't been there before. During their brief, but fiery relationship, Rebecca had denied Stephen nothing, but now she was holding out against him. And it was driving them apart.

Rebecca grew desperate. By now she'd realised her marriage was over. She could never go back to being satisfied with Ron after she'd been with someone as wild and exciting as Stephen. By now, her marriage was beyond saving; she'd well and truly burned her bridges at home – and if she lost Stephen as well she'd be left with nothing. She'd only known him a few short months, but already life without him was becoming unthinkable. She had to keep his interest.

Their love life became even more extreme. Now Stephen would slap her during sex, shoving her around roughly, and she readily went along with it, even when he filmed everything on his mobile phone. But now it wasn't enough. Rebecca could feel Stephen slipping away.

'OK, I'll do it!'

The words came tumbling out before she had time to register she'd said them. And it was worth it for the look on his face. Suddenly the adoration of those early days was back. He was so happy with her again, so in love. Besides, she told herself, it wasn't as if they'd actually go through with it. Lots of people kidded around about killing off husbands or wives, but it didn't make them murderers. Probably Stephen would forget all about it now that he'd got her to agree. He was drinking so heavily by this stage, it was hard to tell how much of what he said was coming straight from the heart and what was straight from the bottle. Maybe all along this had been some sort of test to see how much she loved him.

But Stephen was like the proverbial dog with a bone. Now that Rebecca had said she'd help him kill his wife, he wanted to talk about details. What was the best way to do it? When? Where?

Early on, he ruled himself out of the actual murder. They always suspect the husband first – anyone who'd ever watched a TV police drama knew that. No, he'd have to find himself a foolproof alibi out of the house while Rebecca took care of Jaspal. No one would ever link her to the killing – she'd never even met Jaspal.

'We'll set it up to appear like a burglary that went wrong,' he explained, excitedly.

With a growing sense of unease, Rebecca listened to his plans unfolding. Now that she'd said she'd do it, she couldn't back out – well, not without losing Stephen anyway. But then neither could she go through with killing someone. It was preposterous. All she could do was hope that Stephen tired of the whole thing before she had to break it to him that she was pulling out.

Jaspal Marsh glanced up from the TV at her watch: 10.30 and Stephen was still not home. No doubt he'd have another excuse ready – that he'd met up with friends, had to work late… she'd heard them all a million times before. He must think she was really stupid. She cursed herself for not having listened to her family all those years before. They'd known he was no good for her, but she'd been so blindly in love that she hadn't listened to them. And look at the price she'd paid – thirteen years of watching her husband drink himself silly and flirt with other women, and who knows what more besides behind her back.

'I'm going to leave him,' she'd stormed to friends just a few months before. 'I know he's having an affair.'

But of course Stephen always denied it. 'Don't be silly. You know I love you, Jaz,' he'd tell her whenever she brought anything up.

And, to be honest, with them both working such long hours away from home, they were practically living separate lives anyway, so she'd never carried through her threat. But she knew who Rebecca Harris was. She even had her number logged in her phone. It was under 'B' for 'bitch'.

The knot of tension in Rebecca Harris' stomach was physical, palpable. It weighed her down, sapping her strength, getting in the way of eating and sleeping. Stephen was still not giving up on this murder plan; it was all he ever talked about these days. It was as if he'd casually pushed a cannonball over the top of a hill and now it was thundering down, gaining momentum all the time, and she had no idea how she could stop it.

'It's OK,' she kept telling herself. 'He'll change his mind at the last minute. And even if he doesn't, I'll just tell him I'm not doing it. There's still plenty of time to get out of this.'

If only she could just shift that knot in her stomach, so that she could get a proper night's sleep for once.

'It's all sorted. Everything's set up.' Stephen's eyes were unnaturally bright, his body practically crackling with nervous energy.

Rebecca felt a dull thud of fear somewhere deep inside her. 'What do you mean?' she whispered.

Stephen could hardly contain himself. It was as though someone or something else had taken him over. 'July 28th. It's a Friday night and I know Jaz is going to be at home. We've both got that work do and then I'm going to make sure I've got an alibi straight afterwards. I'll get Jas to leave the door open. You go into the bedroom and stab her in her sleep. It'll be so straightforward – you won't even see her.'

Now the mass in Rebecca's stomach had expanded until it filled her head, pressing down on her brain.

'I can't, Steve,' she faltered.

But then he was clutching her hands tight, his eyes boring into hers. 'Don't you love me, babe?' he was saying. 'Think of our future, you and me together. Do it for us! Don't you want us to be together?'

Of course she did. It was what she wanted more than anything else in the world. He was the first thing she thought about when she woke up and the last thing on her mind before she dropped off to sleep. But how could he ask her to do that, to risk everything?

But Stephen could tell she was wavering and so he stepped up the pressure, barraging her with calls and texts, painting a picture of the fantastic future they'd have once she was divorced from Ron and Jaspal was gone for good. He knew where Rebecca's weakness was – her little boy, and he shamelessly played on that.

'I'd bring him up like he was my own,' he told her, in a phone call. 'We'd be a proper family.'

For Rebecca Harris, who dreamed of starting afresh, this time with a match made for love, rather than for security, this was exactly what she'd been hoping for. They'd be together, all three of them, and her son would have the kind of lifestyle she'd never be able to give him on her own, or if Stephen divorced his wife.

And if she had any lingering thoughts about telling Stephen she'd changed her mind, his next statement soon chased them out of her head. 'If you don't do this, I'll know you don't really love me,' he warned her. 'Then we're finished.'

Rebecca didn't know if she'd want to go on living without Stephen in her life. It was as though he'd got into her skin, as if he ran in her very blood. She'd be a non-person without him, the walking dead.

'I'll do anything for you,' she told him, wretchedly.

28 July 2006 was a Friday and also payday, and the staff at the 118 118 call centre were in a celebratory mood as they gathered after work in a city centre bar. Well, all except Stephen Marsh and Rebecca Harris.

The couple were standing away from the rest of the group and talking animatedly in low voices. By now, the other employees were all used to seeing Stephen and Rebecca whispering together. They were both married to other people but you didn't need to be Sherlock Holmes to work out what was going on between them. Usually there was a lot of flirtatious banter with those two, but tonight both seemed preoccupied with something. Stephen was doing a lot of talking, and Rebecca looked paler than normal, as if she hadn't been sleeping well.

'I can't believe she let me down!' Stephen was ranting about his former mistress, Natalie Yemm. He'd asked her if he could stay the night at her place and at first she'd said yes. Even though he'd ended their relationship the previous October when he started seeing Rebecca, they'd stayed friendly – but now she was saying she'd had second thoughts, just when he needed her most.

'Pick up the phone, for God's sake!' he muttered under his breath as he dialled her mobile yet again, trying to persuade her to change her mind. But there was no reply. Nor was she responding to any of his texts.

For the first time, Rebecca allowed herself a small surge of hope. Without an alibi for Stephen, they'd have to abort the whole plan. Sure, he'd be angry for a bit, but after a few drinks here with all their mates, he'd calm down. Maybe he'd even have reconsidered the whole thing by the next morning.

But even now he was scrolling through the contacts book on his mobile phone. Next on his list of potential alibis was Julie Owens, yet another ex-lover. And when that also proved fruitless, he approached a male friend of his. Bingo!

'We're on!' he told Rebecca, excitedly.

The leaden mass in her stomach swelled until it was everywhere, pressing down on every part of her, leaving her unable to think, unable to breathe.

'There's still time to change my mind,' she told herself. 'I can still pull out any time I like.'

As their co-workers began to disperse, Stephen and Rebecca found themselves outside the bar.

'Just do this, and tomorrow we could be starting a new life together,' Stephen urged, pressing his mistress's hand tightly.

Rebecca could hardly speak. Now, the feeling of nausea that had been slowly building over the evening was threatening to overwhelm her and something strange was happening to her brain. It was as though she could register what Stephen was saying to her but it wasn't quite going in. She felt removed from reality; as though she was sitting apart from herself, but watching herself go through the motions of living and breathing.

Settling in behind the steering wheel of her Mazda, she could see her hand turn the ignition key, and she dutifully looked in the mirror before pulling out, but it still felt like someone else was doing all those things, someone separate. And it was that same separate person who turned the car away from her normal route home to Clos Rhedyn in Cwmrhydyceirw, Morriston, and towards Gorseinon. She was just going to drive past the house, she told herself; she wasn't actually going to do anything.

In the Potters Wheel Pub in Swansea, Stephen's friend Andy was getting fed up. Why had Stephen made such a big fuss about meeting up tonight and asked to stay over if all he was going to do was sit there, sending text messages? He'd already sent several to one number.

Right now he was sending one to his wife. As his fingers punched the letters on his keypad, Stephen's face bore an expression of intense concentration mixed with something else. Excitement? Anticipation? Dread?

He was having a drink with a friend, he told her, but would be home later. 'Just leave the front door open and I'll get a lift home. Love you. xxx'.

Of course, what she didn't know was that by failing to lock the front door from the inside as she normally did, Jaspal was effectively signing her own death warrant.

Rebecca Harris swung the Mazda into Howard's Way, Gorseinon. Such a classy neighbourhood, so peaceful and orderly – it would be a great place for a child to grow up, the streets quiet enough to ride bikes or play football safely. Even now, well after midnight, it didn't feel threatening at all. You just couldn't imagine anything bad happening in a place like this.

As she parked outside number 25, Rebecca's phone beeped. Another text from Stephen, promising her that the front door would be open, and that everything would be straightforward. 'You can do it,' he urged. 'You are strong enough.'

But Rebecca wasn't feeling especially strong now. Her heart was thudding so hard that it felt like her ribcage might shatter under the pressure, but her mind was still disassociated, observing her own actions as if watching a character on TV.

Of course she wasn't actually going to go through with it. She was still just play-acting, getting an idea of how it would feel to approach Stephen's home, to really be about to kill someone...

Thud, thud, thud... Rebecca watched her own hand close around the door handle. Click. The door was unlocked, just as Stephen had promised. Silently, she let herself into the hall, starting as something came towards her through the darkness.

For a split second, she froze, every muscle tensed, each nerve tingling. Then she relaxed, releasing the breath she hadn't even been aware she was holding. It was only Bwbach. The old dog, recognising her from previous visits, ambled forwards to greet her, tail wagging, delighted to have some company in the quiet of the night.

As the dog nuzzled her hand, for a few seconds Rebecca stood motionless, listening for any noises from upstairs. Nothing.

Softly, she edged down the hall, remembering all those other times she'd been there before with Stephen, barely managing to get through the front door before ripping one another's clothes off, desire getting the better of caution in this Neighbourhood Watch community. How different it all felt tonight, alone in the unfamiliar darkness, an intruder rather than a guest.

Creeping into the kitchen, she made her way to the knife block on the counter. Even though it was pitch black, she knew exactly where to find it, of course. She'd watched Stephen numerous times as he ran his fingers over the knife handles, weighing up which one to choose before pulling out the knife he'd want them to use in bed. This time too he'd made the selection for her, sending her a text with instructions to pick out the biggest knife, the one with the 8-inch blade they'd used so many times before during sex. The knife felt familiar as Rebecca held it loosely in her hand. Better the devil you know, and all that, she thought…

Jaspal Marsh tossed fitfully in the double bed she shared with her husband. Though it was late, she just couldn't sleep. That evening, she'd tried her best to relax, talking to a relative on the phone, vegging out on the sofa in front of *Big Brother*, but still she couldn't shake off a vague sense of unease.

It wasn't to do with being alone in the house. Really, Stephen was out so much these days, she ought to be used to being on her own by now. And if the two of them were ever to split up, this was something she was going to have to accustom herself to.

Thinking she might have heard something downstairs, Jaspal lay very still, listening intently. Then she relaxed as she recognised the rhythmic thud of Bwbach's tail hitting the wall. The old dog must be dreaming of chasing rabbits or something. She'd been worried for a moment, though. Honestly, the next time Stephen told her to leave the door unlocked, she was just going to refuse. It just put her on edge and it wasn't fair. Why should she be the one to lose sleep just because he was out enjoying himself? Next time she'd lock it and he could just sleep outside on the doorstep for all she cared.

Thud, thud, thud! Rebecca's heart sounded so loudly in her ears, she was sure Stephen's wife would be able to hear it. She still couldn't quite believe it was her, creeping up the stairs in someone else's house, knife in hand. Surely it was a scene out of a low-budget horror film, not real life – certainly not *her* life. Soon, any second now, she'd wake up from whatever trance she was in and stop what she was doing, horrified at how far she'd gone. She imagined the relief of finding herself outside that house, not caught red-handed breaking into someone else's home, not a potential murderess, just plain Rebecca Harris who'd almost let things get out of hand but had come to her senses just in time.

All of a sudden, the mobile phone she'd been carrying along with the knife lit up. A message: from Stephen, of course.

'Do it. Just do it!' read the text.

She had her instructions.

This time Jaspal was sure there had been a noise but she didn't have time to think about it before the door to the bedroom inched open. If she had been expecting a balaclava-clad burglar then she was very wrong. The person peering uncertainly into the dark bedroom was a young woman. She had something in her hand, something long and thin that glinted where it caught the shaft of moonlight seeping in through the drawn curtains.

Jaspal knew she didn't have much time. If she stayed where she was, she'd be attacked in bed. All she had going for her now was the element of surprise.

'Aaaaaargh!'

Jumping up from the bed, she flew at the intruder, screaming at the top of her lungs.

Rebecca was terrified. She'd been expecting to find a sleeping victim, but instead here was this shrieking banshee tearing at her skin and clothes, pushing her backwards against the chest of drawers. Without pausing to think, she lunged forward with the knife, again and again and again...

'It's not me,' she kept thinking to herself as she felt the other woman grow weaker and then slump to the ground, the knife still buried up to its hilt in her chest. 'This isn't me doing this, it's someone else. This nightmare is happening to someone else.'

She just caught a glimpse of Jaspal Marsh's glassy, staring eyes before she raced headlong down the stairs, thoughts of her son and Stephen jostling through her head.

Flinging open the front door, she ignored Bwbach's reproachful whine as she fled without a goodbye pat, gulping in the fresh night air. Back in the car and speeding away from the house, she felt a mixture of dread and fear and exhilaration. At one level she knew she'd done something so monumental that her life would never be the same again, but on another level, she was just so glad to be free of that house, with its suffocating darkness, where spectres came flying out of nowhere, scratching at your clothes and pulling at your hair.

Her fingers were still trembling from the adrenaline and the fear when she typed out a message to her lover, using their pre-agreed code to let him know it was all done.

'She screamed and fought – I'm shaking so much.'

Rebecca wanted reassurance. She wanted to know Stephen was pleased with her, that all she'd been through and all she'd risked had been worth it because it had won her his approval and his love. She wasn't disappointed.

From his friend's house, where he'd sat up playing computer games after coming back from the pub, making sure his alibi stuck, Stephen Marsh sent her a congratulatory text message: 'You're a star,' he wrote. 'I love you.'

In the master bedroom at 25 Howard's Way, where Jaspal Marsh lay immobile in a pool of blood on the floor, her mobile phone beeped unheard. There was a message coming in, adding to the already crowded inbox.

'Can't believe you haven't called me,' Stephen Marsh had written. 'Love you.'

The following morning, Rebecca was still shaking, although in her mind, she was already distancing herself from what she'd done. Up by six in the morning, she'd completed three loads of washing by the time her husband woke up, but she still couldn't shake off the feeling of being unclean, soiled.

'Everything will be OK now,' she told herself firmly, lighting yet another cigarette, although normally she rarely smoked. 'Stephen and I will be together. I've done everything he asked; I've proved myself to him.'

She kept thinking of the message he'd sent her. He'd be so proud of her for putting their future first. She couldn't wait to see him. Everything would fall into place as soon as they were together again.

But when she drove to pick him up for work as they'd arranged, it was a different story. Rather than throwing his arms around her and comforting her, as she'd hoped he would, Stephen was standoffish, distant even. Rebecca couldn't understand it. He'd come straight from his friend's house without going home so it wasn't as if he was in shock from seeing his wife's body. She just didn't get why he was being so cold – after all she'd done, all she'd been through... Of course she wasn't expecting them to be together right away. She knew there'd be a difficult period while he arranged the funeral and everything. All she wanted was a bit of warmth and understanding to wipe the image of Jaspal Marsh's glazed, unseeing eyes from her head.

'What's wrong?' she asked, miserably, as her passenger sat staring at the road ahead, his hands in his lap.

Stephen shrugged unresponsively, refusing to meet her gaze.

'Talk to me,' she begged.

But he wasn't in the mood for talking. Nor did he return the pressure when she tried to hold his hand, or lean over to kiss her deeply as he'd always done before. When he finally did turn to face her, it was as if someone had switched off the love in his eyes, leaving them shuttered and illegible.

'I'll see you later then,' he said. And then he was gone.

Once again, Rebecca Harris was left alone with her thoughts and her memories, and the glassy-eyed ghost she was trying so hard to keep at bay. This wasn't how it was supposed to be.

That whole day, she tried to concentrate on her work, but she was like an automaton as she answered calls. She was OK as long as she concentrated on the caller and the question, but every now and then a wave of shock would come over her as she remembered what she'd done. Looking round her, she wondered how it could possibly be real. Everything else was so normal – the staff, the phones, even the potted plants. How could the world just potter on as if it were just an ordinary day when something so earth shattering had happened? Wouldn't it all be different? Wouldn't you be able to tell?

'How are you feeling?' she asked Stephen, when he got in the car at the end of the day, ready for a lift home. Again, he wouldn't meet her eyes; again, he just brushed off the question, unwilling to enter into conversation.

He was just in shock, like she was, she told herself. And he was probably steeling himself for what would happen when he went home.

Driving towards Gorseinon, Rebecca's hands clutched the

steering wheel tightly. These were the same roads she'd driven down just the night before, and yet it seemed like a lifetime ago. Now the woman who'd sat behind the wheel while her lover bombarded her with texts, who'd had the option to pull out any time she liked and hadn't appreciated what a luxury that was, seemed like a different person.

Rebecca was fast realising just how much she'd lost. Dropping Stephen off near his home, she felt an overwhelming urge to grab onto him and not let go. She would force him to tell her he still loved her, to reassure her that everything was going to be just as he'd promised. She couldn't bear the blankness in his expression. He was looking at her as though she was nothing to him, as if she was worse than nothing. Didn't he realise how much she'd done for him, for them?

As she watched him walk away from the car in the direction of his home, once again Rebecca felt that crushing weight in her stomach as an agonising thought occurred to her. Might this be the last time she'd ever see him? Had it all been for nothing?

Back home with Ron and her little boy, Rebecca was taciturn and even more irritable than normal. She didn't want to talk to her husband; she didn't want to play at being a fun, happy mummy. All she wanted to do was sit with her mobile phone in her hand, waiting for news from Stephen.

Would the police have fallen for his story about a burglary gone wrong? Had she been seen leaving the house? She wanted to call him so badly, but she didn't dare in case the police were there with him.

By now it was starting to sink in just how huge a thing she'd just done. Sure, she'd made mistakes in her life before – marrying Ron had been one of them – but never any that she couldn't put right again. Slowly she was beginning to realise that this weight she'd been carrying around inside her for the last few weeks, and the panic washing over her in waves since the previous night were now with her for life.

What the hell had she done?

By the next morning, she was a nervous wreck. When the police rang the door bell, wanting to talk to her about the mysterious death of her lover's wife she hardly had the energy to act surprised.

'I went straight home after the work party,' she told them, weakly. 'I've no idea what happened to her.'

But the police, unsurprisingly, simply weren't buying it, particularly when they scrutinised CCTV footage from Friday night in Swansea City Centre and saw Rebecca's car heading in the opposite direction to the one she'd described.

When they came back to Rebecca's house on the Monday after the murder, it was with a warrant for her arrest.

On 2 April 2007, after just two and a half hours, the jury of eight women and four men announced to a packed Swansea Crown Court that they had reached a unanimous verdict in the case of Stephen Marsh.

Over the past seventeen days, the twelve jurors had heard evidence from Rebecca Harris describing how she'd murdered Jaspal Marsh while acting on direct instructions from the victim's husband. They'd heard from police who had a record of the large volume of texts between Rebecca and Stephen on the night of the murder. They'd heard from Stephen's girlfriends, one of whom claimed to have talked to him about murdering his wife. And they'd viewed shocking footage from Stephen's mobile phone of Rebecca Harris writhing on a bed while being sliced with a knife.

On the other hand, they'd also heard Stephen express his deep, abiding love for murdered Jaspal. 'She was going to be my wife forever,' he'd told the court, assembling his handsome features into an appropriate expression for a grieving widower. He'd always managed to get women to agree to anything he asked. Now, with a jury where women outnumbered men two to one, he was putting his charm to the ultimate test.

Rebecca Harris and the other women had been silly mistakes, he confessed, holding his hands up like a naughty boy caught smoking behind the bike shed. They hadn't meant anything. In fact, he had 'no opinion' of Rebecca now and was trying to block her out of his mind.

The jury also heard Stephen blame alcohol for the 'catastrophic memory loss' that caused him to blank out the texts he'd received from Rebecca Harris on the night of the murder. As for those he'd sent her, well, she'd just misinterpreted them.

Stephen Marsh held up his hands to being an alcoholic, he admitted being a womaniser with a penchant for very rough sex, but he flat-out denied being a murderer.

Whatever way the verdict went, it was all over for Rebecca Harris. Already she had confessed to murdering Jaspal and she knew she was going to prison for a very long time. She'd done it all for love, only to have the man of her dreams throw her to the lions in the most public and humiliating way.

She wanted revenge. And when the jury returned its verdict on Stephen Marsh, she got it.

'Guilty!'

In May 2007, Rebecca Harris and Stephen Marsh were back in court to be sentenced for the murder of Jaspal Marsh. Stephen Marsh, who'd tried so hard to wriggle out of any blame, was sentenced to eighteen years in prison for masterminding the murder, while Rebecca Harris received twelve years for carrying it out.

Anyone in court during that trial would be left with one abiding, haunting image - of a woman, tied to a bed while a knife sliced through her flesh.

A relationship rooted in power and in pain carries within it from the start the seed of its own self-destruction. Unfortunately, in the case of Stephen Marsh and Rebecca Harris, it was someone else who would eventually pay the ultimate price for a twisted desire, gone out of control.

## CHAPTER 2

# THE KEN AND BARBIE KILLERS

### KARLA HOMOLKA AND PAUL BERNARDO

Flicking back her long blonde hair, Karla Homolka flashed a wide, exuberant smile at the video camera, showing a row of even teeth as white as the polo-necked sweater she was wearing to keep out the winter chill.

It was 23 December 1990 and the kind of night in this part of Canada where your breath seemed to freeze before it even left your mouth, as you scurried between your front door and car, hoping against hope that the lock wouldn't be frozen shut, forcing you to spend more agonising minutes outdoors, your skin flayed raw by the biting wind.

However, inside the Homolkas' chaotic four-storey home on 61 Dundonald Street in the St Catherine's area of Ontario, just a few miles from the border with North America, the heating was cranked up to the max and pretty, curvy Karla was determined not to let the bleak weather affect what was shaping up to be a fantastic Christmas.

The whole Homolka clan was downstairs in the den, watching the TV, taking silly footage on the video camera, enjoying a few drinks and generally doing what most families do when it's two days before Christmas and too cold to go anywhere.

The three blonde Homolka girls – Karla, 20, Lori, 19, and Tammy, 15 – were in typically high spirits, but Karla was on particularly good form. She'd always loved Christmas: it appealed to the part of her nature that would always stay a little girl; that still loved cuddly toys and heart-shaped stickers and posters of cute baby animals. But this Christmas was going to be more special than ever and the reason for that was lounging on the den floor, shaking with laughter as he tried to keep the video camera steady: her boyfriend and soul mate, 26-year-old Paul Bernardo.

Even now, three years after their first meeting, Karla sometimes still couldn't believe her luck in having found Paul. Like many girls she'd grown up dreaming of the prince who'd whisk her off to a fairytale wedding and now here he was, her very own prince – only more handsome and more charismatic than she'd ever dared imagine. Over 6ft, with piercing blue eyes and light brown hair that fell rakishy over his forehead, Paul Bernardo was everything she wanted.

'Our relationship gets better each day,' Karla gushed a few months earlier in a letter to a girlfriend. 'He's going to make the perfect husband. It looks like all my dreams are coming true, especially the one about finding the best man in the whole world to marry!'

And now she was going to prove to Paul just how much he meant to her. Surveying the cosy family scene, with the Christmas tree in the corner of the room and her sisters and parents and Paul laughing and joking, Karla hugged her mounting nervous excitement to herself. Tonight she was going to give her beloved Paul the best present ever, the one he'd been asking and begging for, but almost given up hope of ever getting.

But the clean-cut, handsome accountant's dearest desire wasn't, as you might guess, a new suit to add to his collection of sharp work-wear, nor the latest album from one of his favourite rappers. What Paul Bernardo most wanted for Christmas, and what his devoted petite girlfriend with the big smile was determined to give him in just a few hours was 15-year-old Tammy Homolka, drugged unconscious and ready to be raped.

Dorothy and Karel Homolka had always had high hopes for their oldest daughter. Strikingly attractive and academically bright, Karla had the potential to be whatever she wanted to be. And if they were disappointed when she shelved any thought of college to work full time in a local vet's clinic, they weren't about to lose sleep over it. It was still a good job, and to a couple who'd started their married life living in trailer parks, anything that brought in a regular paycheck and offered opportunities for advancement was a step in the right direction.

The Homolkas were thrilled the first time Karla brought her

new boyfriend home. Well-spoken, with a ready smile and a promising career at one of the country's best known accountancy firms, Paul Bernardo was everything they could have hoped for. Of course, when the young couple described how they'd met in Toronto, where Karla was at a pet-industry convention and Paul was out on the town with a buddy, they left out the bit where they'd gone directly back to Karla's hotel and had noisy sex for hours in the very same room where her roommate and Paul's friend were trying in vain to get to sleep.

As the couple grew closer, with Paul making the two-hour trip from his home in Scarborough to St Catherines several times a week, the Homolkas jokingly began to refer to him as their 'weekend son'. If Karla occasionally seemed a little too eager to please, well, that was no bad thing for a girl who'd primarily thought of herself for most of her life. And if Paul sometimes appeared overly controlling, again it wouldn't do any harm for Princess Karla to learn that she couldn't get her own way all the time. No, all in all, Paul Bernardo was just what Karla Homolka needed and her parents were only too delighted to welcome him into their slightly shabby but comfortable family home.

Messing around by the pool which had somehow been squeezed into the otherwise cramped back yard, Paul and Karla looked every inch the golden couple. Both effortlessly attractive and brimming with the confidence that comes with youth and beauty, they seemed made to be together. The love notes that passed endlessly between them and pet names they used for one another just further enhanced the impression that they belonged to some elite club with just two lucky members. No wonder Tammy, just 12 when Karla first met Paul, idolised the pair of them. And Paul, to his credit, lavished her with brotherly attention, relishing the feeling of being looked up to and adored.

But beneath the shiny surface, handsome, too-good-to-be-true Paul Bernardo was hiding some ugly secrets. When he left his parents' home in Scarborough every morning in his crisp white shirt and respectable dark suit, briefcase swinging lightly from his hand, he was closing the front door on a family history he'd do anything to forget. Despite his outward confidence and the impression he gave of having the world on a plate, his early life had been anything but easy.

Sure, the Bernardos didn't lack for material stuff – there were the smart clothes, the new bikes, the pool in the back garden… But love? Affection? Nurturing? Those things were in very short supply.

The man Paul had thought of as his father – at least until his mother had told him a few years before in a fit of rage that he was actually the product of an affair with an ex-boyfriend – was an out and out creep. Accountant Ken Bernardo, already unmasked as a peeping Tom, had spent his free time roaming Paul's childhood neighbourhood looking for women to spy on. He'd also sexually abused Paul's older sister, Debbie, and would go on to serve time in jail for doing the same to Debbie's own daughter.

At best, Paul's mother, Marilyn, had a fragile grip on reality. During his teens, she'd holed up in a dark basement room, rarely coming out to supervise him or his older siblings, or to tend to the increasingly filthy house. As Marilyn, suffering from an undiagnosed thyroid condition, piled on the weight, Ken Bernardo heaped scorn, ridicule and contempt on his wife. His occasional visits to the basement for sexual gratification did nothing to improve relations between the couple but instead instilled in him a sense of humiliation and self-loathing which he invariably transferred back to his wife, stepping up the insults and vitriol.

According to local legend his 'father' referred to Marilyn as 'it' while Paul preferred the moniker 'slut'. Even before the revelations about his paternity, there was never much in the way of mother-son bonding, but afterwards there was nothing but undisguised mutual antipathy, and Paul rarely bothered to hide his disdain for Marilyn and the way she lived.

What Marilyn Bernardo taught her younger son was that women are cheaters, that they're unclean and worthy only of contempt. And what Ken Bernardo taught him was that sex is something dirty that happens furtively in darkness and has everything to do with power and control and nothing to do with love. What the relationship between the two of them taught him was that marriage is about abuse rather than equality, about self-gratification rather than mutual support, lust rather than happiness.

That's a hell of a legacy, wouldn't you say?

Perhaps unsurprisingly given his background, Paul had had problems with his early sexual relationships. His girlfriends, initially attracted by his wholesome good looks and easy charm, tended to go off him rapidly once he revealed his predilection for violent, perverted sex.

'Come on, it'll be fun,' he'd coax, trying to make the appeal in his blue eyes as irresistible as possible. But one look at the rope with which he was intending to tie them up or a hint of what he wanted them to do with the empty wine bottle on the table was usually enough to set alarm bells clanging.

But Paul Bernardo, who grew up in a house of deprivation, had vowed to deny himself nothing. If he couldn't make women do what he wanted voluntarily, he'd just get them to do it some other way. By the time he met Karla at the age of 23, Paul had already started sexually assaulting women. Lurking in the shadows at night, he'd single out a lone woman, often walking home from a bus stop, and follow her. Brandishing a knife, he'd grab her from behind, touching her roughly, and getting a kick from the fear in her face as she realised, with sudden horror, what was happening. Other people's terror excited him. In his view women deserved neither sympathy nor empathy. Anyone who was not a virgin was necessarily a slut; that was his philosophy.

But Karla was different. While sleeping with him meant she was still a 'slut' according to Paul's warped way of thinking, she was such an enthusiastic one that he couldn't resist her. Where other girlfriends had been repulsed by his inability to separate pain from pleasure – more specifically *their* pain, *his* pleasure – Karla seemed to delight in it.

'I'll do whatever you want to,' she'd murmur, looking up at

him from those knowing, heavy-lidded eyes that seemed so incongruous in her fresh, 17-year-old face.

'Fetch the handcuffs,' she'd urge him. 'Tell me what to do! You're my king.'

No wonder Paul Bernardo, powerful lord and master of his own universe, was smitten. All his life he'd been driven to dominate – over his squalid surroundings, his dysfunctional family… In Karla Homolka he'd not only met someone he could dominate completely and fully, but who also enjoyed it, even seemed to egg him on to more extreme acts. Less than a month after their first fateful meeting, Karla sent him a card that read: 'Roses are red, violets are blue, there's nothing more fun than a pervert like you!' Encouraged, Paul decided to broach the subject of the sexual assaults he'd been carrying out.

'How would you feel about me if I was a rapist?' he asked his new cherubic, blonde teenage girlfriend.

'That'd be cool,' she replied.

It was a match made in heaven. Or hell.

The one problem with Karla, Paul's biggest bone of contention, was that she wasn't a virgin when they met. This enraged him. How could he fully dominate her when she'd been 'owned' before? For a bastard child who'd never felt he rightfully belonged in his family, who'd gone to school in hand-me-downs from his older siblings, ownership was essential. He didn't want a second-hand car – he wanted a shiny new one. And he didn't want a girlfriend who'd been 'broken in' by someone else. It was the same virgin/slut argument. No one wanted to sleep with a slut, so the only other option was a virgin. Of course the Catch 22 was that, by sleeping with a virgin, he would automatically convert her into a slut, which would in turn make her a deserving target for his sadistic abuse and contempt.

For a while it seemed the issue of Karla's virginity, or lack of it, would drive a permanent wedge between the perfect couple.

'I'm so sorry for what I've done,' Karla wrote in a heartfelt letter to her suddenly cold and wavering lover. 'You're the best person I've ever loved in my life... You deserve someone perfect, someone who is truly yours.' Then came the chilling phrase: 'There are no perfect people in the world: if you find your virgin, there will be something wrong with her.'

Of course there would be. As Oscar Wilde once said, each man kills the thing he loves. By deflowering a virgin, in his own warped mind, Paul would be creating a slut. Karla was more perceptive than she realised.

Paul quickly relented in the face of Karla's abject remorse and grief, and she was once again reinstated as his princess, his cute little Karla-Curls, but the experience taught her two important lessons: one, that virginity was very, very important to her incredible new boyfriend, and two, that she never wanted to be without him and she'd do anything – *anything* – to keep him.

While Karla struggled with finishing school and keeping her demanding lover satisfied, Paul had other things on his mind. Not satisfied with just scaring lone females, he'd graduated to violent rape. Over a period of a few months he sadistically attacked women and girls, some as young as 15, raping them repeatedly and brutally, and, in what became his unique modus operandi, forcing them to repeat demeaning and degrading phrases praising him for his sexual prowess and decrying their own worthlessness.

'I love you,' he'd have them say, again and again, as he raped them from behind, the blade of his knife pressing into their backs. 'I'm a little slut.'

Hearing their terrified voices stammer out the words to his own twisted script, he felt a surge of pure power and vindication; his breaths came hotter and faster as he thrilled to the knowledge of his own potency. He was the king, he was entitled to have his sexual desires satisfied… And besides, these women were whores anyway – just listen to them!

But although he never bothered to disguise himself, and although the traumatised victims repeatedly gave police accurate descriptions of their young clean-cut attacker, Paul Bernardo was never apprehended. Even when a composite picture of the man who'd become known as 'The Scarborough Rapist' was released and people at work began to tease him about the similarities, no one seriously suspected him. Why would a man who had everything going for him, not to mention a gorgeous girlfriend who hung on his every word, need to rape anyone? The idea was ludicrous.

Of course, the longer he carried on getting away with his sick crimes, the more convinced he became of his own superiority and invincibility. They couldn't catch him for the simple reason that he was too quick for them, too clever. He could do anything he wanted, and, more to the point, he had the right to do so. In his eyes, he was above the law of normal men – he was in a league of his own.

As his confidence in his own supremacy skyrocketed, so too did his need to have this fact recognised by the people around him, particularly Karla. He devoted himself to training his young girlfriend. Karla, in thrall to her older, more sophisticated lover and still reeling from the shock of having his affections suddenly withdrawn from her, determined to be everything he wanted.

Sexually, she denied him nothing, whole-heartedly joining in, even as his demands became increasingly disturbing. She cheerfully 'performed' on camera while he videoed their sex sessions, directing her every move, and she encouraged him in his fantasies, where inevitably domination and desire invariably went hand in hand.

When one of Karla's school friends visited, she was shocked to see a hand-written note pinned to her friend's bedroom wall. In her childish, looping writing, Karla had compiled a list of ways to improve herself in order to make herself into the 'perfect' girlfriend.

'Don't talk back to Paul,' the formerly assertive, feisty teen had written. 'Always smile when you're with Paul. Be a perfect girlfriend for Paul. If Paul asks for a drink, bring him one quickly and happily. Remember you're stupid. Remember you're ugly. Remember you're fat.'

Under Paul's 'guidance', Karla changed not only her

demeanour but also her image, swapping her previously untamed permed hair for a sleeker style and her individualistic clothes for more demure, conservative look.

But any misgivings her friends or family might have had about her sudden transformation were quickly quelled in the face of her obvious adoration. She was forever telling people how happy the two of them were, and how good Paul was to her, how lucky she was to have found him. And when they got engaged in 1989, you'd have thought Prince Charming himself had asked her to marry him.

'I'd do anything for that man,' she'd gush to her envious friends, as they pored over wedding magazines and catalogues. 'I never want to lose him.'

No one, not even Karla herself, could have had any idea then just how much she would be called upon to do to keep from losing her domineering boyfriend and how dearly it would cost her.

While Paul was congratulating himself on his own cleverness in continuing to evade capture, despite sexually attacking over a dozen women, and in successfully moulding Karla into his own personal sex slave and fan club combined, he couldn't shake off his low-level anger at her for not having saved herself for him.

'I don't love you,' he'd frequently hiss at her, reminding her that she was a slut for having lost her virginity before she met him. 'You disgust me!'

To Karla, by now conditioned to need his love and approval, desperate not to relinquish the status that being one half of the 'golden couple' afforded, this was an unbearable blow.

'Tell me what to do,' she'd beg him. 'I'll do anything. You're my king. Tell me how to make you love me again.'

Offering herself to him, she'd tell him all the things she wanted to do with him in bed – and out of it: the dressing up as a schoolgirl, the bondage, the home-made X-rated movies… all the stuff she knew excited him. But all too often Paul would look down at her with the same expression of disdain he'd so often seen his 'father' Ken use with his mother. 'I don't want you,' he'd all but spit. 'You're soiled goods! I want a virgin, someone untouched – someone like Tammy.'

By the time she was 15, Paul's feelings for Karla's little sister had gone from affection to obsession. Like her older sibling, Tammy was lively, extrovert and pretty, but unlike Karla, she was still sexually inexperienced. Paul grew increasingly fixated on being the one to take her virginity.

Karla, meanwhile, was overrun with conflicting emotions. On one hand, she felt protective of her younger sister, but on the other she was deeply jealous of her and of the hold she had over Paul. Tammy, proud of the bond she had with her sister's cute, handsome boyfriend, was happy to spend time with him, flirting with him in that innocent, unknowing way that teenage girls, not yet unaware of their sexual power, sometimes do.

With growing uneasiness, Karla looked on. Could her little sister really steal her man away from her? It wasn't fair. If she'd known she'd meet someone as incredible as Paul, of course she'd have waited for him, but she was being punished for something she could never have anticipated, while Tammy could do no wrong. What could she do to prove to Paul how sorry she was and how much she loved him?

The answer was simple: she could give Tammy to Paul.

By this stage, late in 1990, Karla was working at a veterinary clinic where she had easy access to powerful tranquilisers. Paul was sure they could drug Tammy's drink with a sedative that would mean he could rape her without her feeling a thing, or even waking up. At first Karla had dismissed his outlandish and perverted fantasy, but when he kept pestering her, she'd started to think more about it. Careful research convinced her that ground-up Halcion tablets would be undetectable in a drink and enough to render someone unconscious, while a cloth soaked in halothane held over the mouth would keep them that way too.

With Karla's assistance, Paul could have sex with Tammy and when she woke up the next morning, she'd be none the wiser and they could all go on as if nothing had happened. Reluctant at first, Karla came to believe it was a win-win situation on so many levels – Paul would stop obsessing about Tammy's virginity and using it against her, it would reduce the chances of Paul and Tammy actually starting up a consenting sexual relationship at some point in the future, and it would strengthen the bond between herself and Paul.

When she told him what she'd found out, and agreed to steal the drugs, Paul was delighted with her and Karla basked in his approval and approbation. Once again she was his cute, clever Karla-Curls, his perfect girlfriend, his soul mate.

Tammy would never know anything about it, Karla convinced herself. It wasn't doing her any real harm, was it? And Paul would be so very grateful to her, it would all be worth it.

December 1990 was the perfect opportunity. Not only would the Homolka family be spending a lot of time together, most likely drinking quite heavily, but this would also count as the ideal Christmas present for Paul.

Accustomed by now to focusing on her man's happiness above all others, and wary of provoking his displeasure, which had started to show itself in physical violence, Karla didn't dwell too much on any potential problems or threats to her little sister's wellbeing. Instead, she indulged Paul in constructing endless fantasies about the forthcoming rape, fuelling his anticipation and mounting excitement. Lucky Tammy would be introduced to sex by a master, the couple agreed. What a shame she'd never know how good it had been!

But of all the twisted scenarios that the couple came up with, discussing the rape of Tammy Homolka, nothing would match the actual horror of the events that unfolded on the evening of 23 December 1990.

At first, it seemed as everything was going to plan. All the Homolkas were drinking quite heavily and although Tammy was still a couple of weeks' shy of her sixteenth birthday, no one was about to deny her a few celebratory cocktails this close to Christmas. As Paul and Karla mixed the drinks, it was easy enough to slip a sprinkling of crushed Halcion into Tammy's glass.

For an agonising few hours, Karla and Paul thought the drug wasn't working. Tammy was relaxed, as they all were, but she didn't seem particularly sleepy. Just when they were beginning to give up hope of being able to put their plan into action, things started to fall into place, however. As Paul and Karla settled down to watch a video in the basement den, the rest of the Homolka clan decided they were ready for bed, all except Tammy, who stayed to watch the movie. That decision was to cost her life.

The film hadn't been playing long when Karla nudged Paul. Tammy, who was lying on the sofa, had fallen asleep. This was their big chance. Karla bent over Tammy, lifting her arm and then dropping it to test how soundly she was asleep. The younger girl didn't stir; she was out cold. So, now for the second part of the plan…

After helping Paul roughly pull up Tammy's shirt and tug her trousers down, Karla swiftly got the halothane and a cloth she'd prepared earlier. While she stood at her sister's head, holding the halothane doused rag over her Tammy's face, Paul acted out every unspeakable, twisted fantasy he'd been imagining over the past weeks and months – all captured by his new video camera so they'd be able to relive the experience again and again.

It was amazing, better than he'd ever envisaged. The knowledge of Tammy's virgin status excited him even more than he'd anticipated. She was all his, no one else could ever say they'd been there before him. He was the man all right: he was King!

Nervously, Karla kept an eye on her sleeping sister. Although she'd been present at numerous animal operations, she had no idea how much halothane she needed to administer to keep Tammy unconscious.

Then all of a sudden, in a departure from the prepared script, Paul ordered Karla to take part in the rape. At first she demurred, particularly when she realised Tammy had her period. But she couldn't deny Paul anything for long and within minutes the camera caught her sexually violating her own sister, following commands from her boyfriend, of course – but looking as if she was enjoying it too.

It was all too much for Paul – he wanted another go. As Karla once again assumed her position holding the drug-soaked cloth over her sister's face, Paul was back to re-enacting the fantasy he'd had for so long.

Then suddenly everything went wrong.

Tammy made a movement and Karla realised she was choking on her own vomit. 'Shit! Do something!' she cried. But Paul, who normally prided himself on being in control of any situation, was panicking.

With a growing sense of foreboding Karla tried to remember what they would do in the veterinary surgery in case of an emergency. Roughly she manoeuvred her unresisting sister until her head was upside down, trying in vain to clear her airways, but nothing seemed to work.

'We've got to get her out of here!'

Karla wasn't thinking straight. This wasn't supposed to have happened. All she could think was that Tammy needed to be taken away from the sofa, and all the evidence of what they'd just done to her, and laid out somewhere they could look after her properly. Trying to quell their panic, the couple dragged the lifeless girl into Karla's bedroom which was just off the den but they quickly realised all their efforts at resuscitation were in vain.

'We need an ambulance. Quick!'

Karla's frantic 911 call betrayed her utter desperation: she hadn't meant for Tammy to be hurt, this wasn't supposed to happen. And yet, while the couple waited for the emergency services to arrive, Karla didn't exactly act the grief-stricken, older sister. As well as washing and re-dressing Tammy, she took the time out to dispose of the halothane and the cloth – and of course the video tape.

The shocked Homolka parents, who'd been woken from their sleep by the ambulance sirens accompanying their youngest daughter to the hospital, left Karla, Paul and Lori at home waiting anxiously for news. A short while later it came, but it wasn't what anyone wanted to hear: Tammy Homolka was declared dead on arrival at the hospital.

The policeman who had stayed behind with Paul, Karla and Lori while Tammy was rushed to hospital was saddled with the unenviable task of breaking the news.

'No, no, *no*!' Paul screamed in anguish, as the reality of Tammy's death sank in. Karla and her only surviving sister clung to each other in mute misery. There was no doubting the genuineness of their grief. And yet, just a short while later, the policeman was stunned to discover Karla about to do a load of washing, cramming the vomit-caked covers on which Tammy had been lying into the washing machine.

'You can't do that,' he told her. 'Everything has to stay just as it is.'

Inevitably, there would have to be a postmortem. So much of what had happened seemed strange. Why had a healthy young girl choked after a relatively small amount of alcohol? And why had Paul and Karla dragged her into the bedroom, causing a burn to appear around her mouth?

For an agonising few days, Paul and Karla waited to hear the coroner's ruling. Would they find out that Tammy had been raped? And would they discover evidence of the halothane in her system?

Incredibly, when the results of the autopsy came out, they revealed the official cause of death to be aspiration – fluid on the lungs – caused by Tammy choking on her own vomit, just as Karla and Paul had said.

But even though the couple seemed to have got away Scot-free, they were far from happy. In their own warped way they'd loved Tammy, and more to the point they'd believed they were completely in control. How could things have gone so terribly wrong?

Inevitably, Paul blamed the whole fiasco on Karla.

'You must have given her too much halothane,' he raged at her in private, away from the grieving relatives. 'It was all going so well and then you ruined it, you stupid bitch!'

Even viewing the tape of the attack wasn't the consolation it should have been to Paul Bernardo. Sure, there was all the good stuff at the beginning, showing him and Karla having fun with the unconscious Tammy, but then it all went horribly wrong and no amount of editing was going to change the fact that the script had been completely forgotten and Tammy was dead.

Karla was desperate. She knew Paul was going to continue punishing her for her 'mistake'. She had to make it up to him. Three weeks after Tammy's death, while the Homolka parents were away, trying to come to terms with their grief, Paul kidnapped a girl and brought her back to the Homolka house. While he raped her on the floor of the bedroom, Karla looked on approvingly. Afterwards she cleaned up while he dumped the never-identified girl on a deserted road, leaving her traumatised and bewildered, but nevertheless somehow still alive. Though she would never have believed it then, the 'January Girl' as she became known to the couple was one of the lucky ones.

A few days later, as if she were commenting on a new joint hobby, Karla suggested she and Paul should kidnap more virgins for his sexual pleasure. 'If you want to do it fifty times more, we can do it fifty times,' she told him. 'We can do it every weekend.'

Even a hardened psychopath like Paul was stumped by that one, but when he asked why the woman to whom he was engaged would voluntarily bring back other girls for him to have sex with, Karla's response was unequivocal: 'Because I love you, because you're the King.'

Not long after, Karla willingly participated in another of

Paul's home-video productions. In this one she dressed up as her dead sister while having sex with Paul, even holding Tammy's photo over her own face, pretending to be the virgin he'd so set his heart on.

'Karla will never know about us,' she boasted to Paul, in her imitation-Tammy voice, on her knees between his legs, never letting herself lapse out of the role she'd so enthusiastically assumed.

Proficient as Karla's play-acting skills doubtlessly were, nothing could alter the fact that she wasn't the real thing, the virginal young girl of Paul's fantasies, however. Once again she decided to make Paul a present of a girl who possessed the one attribute that she herself would never have again. With her sister Tammy dead, Karla remembered a young girl called Jane whom she'd befriended a few years before at the vet's clinic where she worked. Jane would be around 15 now – the perfect age for her nearly 27-year-old fiancé.

By this stage Karla and Paul had moved to their own home on Bayview Drive in upmarket Port Dalhousie, St Catherine's. When Jane arrived there, responding to Karla's invitation to spend a 'girlie' evening together, she immediately fell in love with the smart clapboard house with its spotless grey carpets and jacuzzi. Really, she thought to herself, Karla Homolka was exactly the kind of woman she wanted to be in a few years – well-off, confident, beautiful… And although she had yet to meet Karla's fiancé, who was out for the night, somehow Jane just knew he'd be gorgeous.

The evening was everything the young, impressionable girl could have wanted. She and Karla went into town for dinner and then returned to the house to watch videos and have a few drinks together. And if Jane noticed her drinks seemed to have a funny aftertaste, she certainly wasn't about to say so. She was only 15 and her knowledge of alcohol was very limited. This must be the way it was supposed to taste, and if Karla wasn't complaining, she wasn't about to show her lack of sophistication by mentioning it.

Soon, in an exact re-enactment of the Tammy scenario, Jane was unconscious, which was how Paul found her when Karla called him back early to the house.

'Such a clever girl,' he told her approvingly, once again unable to believe his luck in finding the one woman who was unfazed, even aroused by his unusual sexual appetites.

The rape of Jane followed exactly the same script as that of Tammy, only this time Karla was monitoring the girl's airways as she administered the halothane. Even during the part where she herself took part in the assault, licking her lips lasciviously for the omnipresent video camera, she still kept an eye on the other girl's breathing. This time there were no mishaps, for when Jane woke up the following morning she had a terrible hangover but no recollection of anything after she passed out.

'Nice to meet you,' she said politely, when Karla introduced her to her fiancé, Paul.

Just as she'd thought, he was gorgeous – and so polite and funny too. Karla really did have it all.

But if Karla had been hoping that by procuring Jane for Paul, she'd be able to sustain his interest for a while, she was mistaken. It seemed like the more action he got, the more he wanted, and the greater the level of violence he used.

As 1991 wore on and their wedding planned for 29 June drew ever closer, Karla became increasingly anxious that Paul would tire of her and that he'd abandon their lavish wedding plans and go off with someone else. To her, this was unthinkable. By this stage, she was indoctrinated to think that she needed Paul in her life – in fact, his life and his needs were more important than her own. And for a girl like Karla who'd always made herself her number one that was really saying something. Then there was the wedding – the best champagne, a horse-drawn carriage, the ceremony in a little church on Niagara-on-the-Lake, the fairytale hotel overlooking the Niagara River... even pheasant stuffed with veal. Everything was planned with meticulous detail. She wasn't about to let anything jeopardise her hard work.

So when Paul woke her a couple of weeks before the wedding telling her to stay upstairs as he'd brought home a young girl to play with – someone he'd snatched off the street at knifepoint – Karla didn't make a fuss. Perhaps she thought it would be like the other times, that he'd do his own thing and then return the girl back to the street.

While Karla obediently dozed back off to sleep, seemingly unconcerned about what Paul had just told her, downstairs the terrified Leslie Mahaffy was finally beginning to realise what was happening to her. Just a few hours earlier, she'd been a typically cocky, rebellious 14-year-old, who'd arrived home past her curfew to find the doors of her house locked against her. Her mother had thought she'd teach her a lesson. What she could never have reckoned on was the possibility of her daughter running into someone like Paul Bernardo.

By this time Paul had more or less given up accountancy in favour of the more lucrative but riskier alternative of smuggling cigarettes over the nearby border from the US back into Canada, where they were far more expensive. To help in this new enterprise he had to keep changing the plates on his car, and it was while prowling the streets in nearby Burlington, searching for number-plates to steal, that Paul had run into Leslie.

There are some coincidences that fortuitously send your life spinning in a different, better orbit, and others so cruel they take your breath away. Paul Bernardo wasn't even looking for a victim that night, but Leslie literally walked right into his path. It was his lucky night – and the start of her descent into hell.

'You got any cigarettes?' the 14-year-old asked him, after he'd told her he was casing one of her neighbours' houses to break in.

He smiled at her, playing the part of the loveable rogue to perfection.

'Sure,' he told her. 'They're in my car. Come and get one.'

As he'd just come back from a smuggling expedition, there really were plenty of cigarettes in Paul's car. Also there was the knife he used to force Leslie inside, and the sweater he tied around her head as a blindfold. The terrified youngster got one last look at the familiar streets of her neighbourhood before the whole world went dark.

Back at Paul and Karla's home, Leslie didn't know it yet, but her nightmare was only just beginning. The whole of that first night, Paul 'played' with her – raping her virginally and anally, getting her to give him oral sex... Whatever degrading act he could think of, Paul had Leslie do. And, of course, he videotaped it all. He even videotaped her on the toilet, her evident embarrassment and shame just adding to the thrill he was getting from the whole experience.

When Karla got up the next morning, she was fed up. Not, as you might think, because her fiancé was shut in the spare bedroom with a young girl he'd picked up off the streets two weeks before their wedding. No, the thing that really got to her was that their best champagne glasses were out on the dining room table. What a cheek! She really resented the fact that Paul had used the 'good' glasses with someone else, some stranger at that. It was so disrespectful.

Later that evening, however, Karla had calmed down enough to join the other two. After all, the relationship books all advised marrying couples to find some joint interests and she was determined to start married life on the right foot, supporting her man any way she could. And if his interests happened to lie with brutally raping and assaulting young girls, well, who was she to question it? Best to join in when told, and to enjoy it, because when it came down to it, some of it was fun and it made Paul so happy.

The last thing Karla wanted to do was make Paul angry. There was the big lavish wedding, just days away, to think about and then there was the lifestyle she and Paul led, one that would be impossible on her meagre vet assistant's wages. Plus, the ever-present worry of Paul's unpredictable and increasingly violent temper. When he was fed up, who was it that suffered? Yep, that's right, little old Karly-Curls, that's who! And finally, there was the tape of Tammy's rape. If that ever came to light, Karla would lose everything she held most dear. No, Karla Homolka knew she had everything to gain from standing by her man.

Under the ever-watchful gaze of the video camera, Karla took her turn having sex with Leslie, seemingly oblivious to the other girl's barely disguised terror. Then she got behind the lens as director, holding the camera steady while Paul subjected his young victim to a string of horrifyingly violent assaults.

Leslie's screams didn't really have much affect on Karla. It wasn't as if she could do anything to help her, right? Paul would be so angry if she did anything without his permission – she just couldn't risk him hitting her, or worse still, showing anyone the video of what they'd done to Tammy. Besides, Karla had done her best to make Leslie feel comfortable – asking her questions about her family, her favourite things to do at the weekend... They'd had a nice little chat. Really, if she just relaxed a little, the younger girl might find she actually enjoyed the rough stuff, just as she herself often did.

Did Karla know at that point that the agonising hours Leslie Mahaffy spent as the couple's unwilling sex slave would be the last of her short life? Was she already aware that her own face and Paul's, contorted with desire and flushed with sexual exertion, would be the last the young girl would ever see?

Whatever the case, the outcome remains the same. Some time after being kidnapped and repeatedly raped by both Karla and Paul, Leslie Mahaffy was killed. Later in court each partner would accuse the other of the murder. Paul claimed Karla, jealous of the attention he was lavishing on his new 'toy' and anxious not to be identified, had killed Leslie while he was briefly away from the house. Karla, in turn, claimed Paul had strangled her so she couldn't go to the police.

The matter of the disposal of Leslie's body would be similarly blame-shifted between the couple, with Karla claiming minimal involvement and Paul insisting she was the key player. What's not under dispute is that, following her murder, Leslie's slight 14-year-old body was kept under a shelf in a dark cupboard off the basement, while the couple entertained Karla's parents to a Father's Day meal.

What would Dorothy and Karel have said if they'd known that just beneath the table where they were tucking into a chicken dinner, Leslie Mahaffy's body lay in lonely solitude, growing colder by the minute? Just how might their feelings have changed for their son-in-law to be, who even now sat chatting and joking opposite them? What would they have thought of their eldest daughter, their high-achieving Karla, had they known what secrets she was hiding behind her curtain of blonde hair?

Later, Karla would recall how her mum offered to go down to the basement to fetch some potatoes from the cupboard where Leslie's body lay wrapped in its black plastic shroud.

'No, wait! I'll go!' she'd shrieked as she realised what was happening. Jumping up from her chair, she'd just managed to get to the basement door before her slower-moving mother.

Once Karla's parents had left, again the couple's statements diverge. At some point, Bernardo came up with the idea of cutting Leslie's body up and encasing the parts in cement blocks, which could then be dumped in nearby Lake Gibson. Did Karla, as she was to claim, become so repulsed by the idea that she finally got up the courage to stand up to Paul and refuse to participate, despite having conspicuously failed to do so just hours before, when such firmness could have saved Leslie's life? Or did she, as she was to do again and again, accede to his demands out of a mixture of fear, obsessive devotion and what psychologists would later describe as her innate 'moral vacuity'?

The unavoidable reality is that Leslie's body was brutally dismembered in the couple's basement with a power saw. The fact that no evidence of this was ever discovered, despite meticulous police searches of the house, indicates the whole area must have been shrouded in tarpaulin.

For a few gruesome hours one or both partners concentrated on cutting Leslie's body into pieces, not flinching when the blood sprayed out, or the bones cracked apart. Could Paul Bernardo, increasingly erratic psychopath, have patiently and methodically done all this alone? Or was it, as Paul insisted,

Karla, the experienced veterinary surgeon's assistant, who then washed the individual body parts down before placing them in ten separate plastic rubbish bags? These were then encased in blocks of quick-drying cement, which Paul bought from a local hardware store and dumped from the bridge into the waters of Lake Gibson. With breath-taking arrogance, he would even return the bags of cement he didn't use to the store, signing his name and address on the refund form.

Could one human being really do to another what Paul did to Leslie, possibly with Karla's help? Could one person really slice into another's flesh, cutting bone from bone, tearing tissue apart, watching the blood pool and congeal on surfaces and floors, thick and tacky as carelessly spilled cough medicine? Could a person pick up a young girl's unattached foot and carry it to a sink? What about a hand? A torso? A head? Could a person do all this and still remain sane?

More than a decade on, Canadians would still debate these points.

On 29 June 1991, two weeks after the killing of Leslie Mahaffy, Karla and Paul were married in a ceremony so opulent that people would talk about for weeks and months to come. While the wedding guests tucked into their pheasant and gulped down their champagne, a man fishing with his son at nearby Lake Gibson made a horrifying discovery: a piece of a girl's thigh, partly encased in concrete, lay just beneath the surface of the lake, uncovered by the low tide.

At the end of that day, by the time the radiant bride and her handsome groom had finished their turn around the Niagara hotel grounds in their white horse-drawn carriage and Karla's mother had been congratulated for the hundredth time on how beautiful her daughter looked, and what good fortune she'd had to find a man like Paul, another seven similar blocks had been pulled out of the murky waters. Each one would be found to contain separate body parts: Leslie Mahaffy was back on dry land.

If Karla and Paul had any momentary twinges of remorse for what they'd done or any nagging worries about being found out, they certainly weren't giving any signs of this as they lived it up on their honeymoon in Hawaii. Fellow holidaymakers gazed over at them with a mixture of envy and goodwill. They were so young and attractive, and so obviously in love. These days, of course, you couldn't bet on any marriage outlasting the wedding cake, but there was something about Paul and Karla that made onlookers feel their union would be one of the exceptions. They seemed so well matched, so comfortable together.

Watching Paul and Karla strolling together along the beach, hand in hand, twin fair-haired heads lit up by the sun, no one would have believed that Paul had just made a momentous announcement to Karla, one that would have shocked any other bride into packing her suitcase and fleeing onto the next plane back. He had revealed that he was the Scarborough Rapist.

All the time Paul and Karla were together, right up until they moved into their new home in St Catherine's, Paul had continued his raping spree, causing a wave of fear and panic among women in his locality. So widespread was the terror that the transport company even ordered bus drivers to drop their female passengers as near to their homes as possible in order to foil any attacker targetting the bus stops.

Of course, Paul Bernardo just loved that. The idea that a whole town was afraid to go out after dark because of him just played right up to his megalomaniac fantasies. He was all-powerful, he was the King... everyone was in thrall to him, and no one, but no one, would ever catch him.

Not that the police hadn't come close a couple of times. The drawing-up of a composite picture based on descriptions given by several of the rape victims had led to a flurry of positive identifications. Luckily, hundreds of other men who also fitted the bill had been similarly reported in by ex-wives, girlfriends and neighbours all doing the right thing.

When police, acting on a tip-off from the public, had interviewed Bernardo in November 1990, they'd been unable to reconcile this polite, quietly spoken man, soon to be married to a gorgeous young blonde, with the image they had of the brutal beast who'd ripped apart so many women's lives. He'd readily agreed to give them samples of body fluid, realising perhaps that, as one of hundreds interviewed, they were unlikely to be processed for a very long time, if at all. To the interviewing officers, the amenable, charming Bernardo certainly didn't seem like a man with anything to hide. As he predicted, his samples were caught up in a backlog and remained indefinitely on file.

Back from honeymoon, the new Mr and Mrs Bernardo were

shocked to hear the news that a young girl's body parts had been found in Lake Gibson. Well, that wasn't surprising: everyone in that generally quiet, safe area was appalled.

'You should have known about the tides – you've lived here all your life!' Paul raged at Karla.

Typical! Every little thing that went wrong turned out to be her fault. Karla was getting so fed up with it all… Tired of always walking on eggshells around Paul, fed up with always getting the blame and with his ever-more frequent and violent beatings. It was getting so that she didn't dare say or do anything without Paul's say-so just in case she got it wrong. Karla loved the swanky house and the lifestyle she and Paul enjoyed, and she still loved Paul in the kind of way that an alcoholic loves the booze that's killing them, but sometimes she wished they could be a normal couple, just like everyone else.

But normal was anathema to Paul Bernardo. By this stage he'd committed numerous rapes, had drugged women, tortured them and even murdered them. Still no one suspected a thing. That meant he was above the laws of ordinary men – he was untouchable. He was, as he kept telling the women he brutalised, the King.

And the King wasn't to be content for long with just replaying the Leslie and Tammy video tapes. Within months, Bernardo was restless again. As usual it was Karla's fault. If she had been enough for a man like him, he wouldn't constantly need more. Once again, the couple brought Jane out to 'play', cosying up to the flattered teenager, making her feel special… But all the time they were being so 'nice' to her, Paul was touching her inappropriately or pestering her to have sex with him. When the reluctant and confused girl looked to Karla for help, the older woman would make light of it, or tell Jane what a wonderful guy Paul was, and suggest how she wouldn't mind sharing him. Poor Jane, still ignorant of having been used by the couple before while unconscious, put up with a certain amount of mauling, just so she could stay being friends with Karla whom she still idolised. But she drew the line at sexual intercourse. After all, she was still a virgin – or so she thought.

As Mr and Mrs Paul Bernardo's marriage entered its second year, a few things were gradually changing. More frequently, the young Mrs Bernardo was turning up for work with bags under her eyes, as though she'd had trouble sleeping. Sometimes she also had bruises on her arms, which she explained away by having rough-housed with her dog, Buddy. When questioned, Karla still went to great lengths to tell people just how great her marriage was, and how lucky she was to have found Paul. Visitors to the couple's home, who stumbled across any of the love notes Karla wrote to her husband on an almost daily basis, would wonder at the intensity of feeling the newly-weds seemed to share, even five years after first getting together. But then that was Karla Homolka for you: everything was about putting up a good façade, creating a golden impression other people would envy. It was almost as if she couldn't enjoy her life and the things she had except by seeing the reflection of it in other people's covetous eyes.

Her young, bleached-blond husband was still making his lucrative cigarette smuggling trips across the border from the US. Clean-cut and well spoken, no one ever stopped him. And on the days when he wasn't doing that, he was holed up in his 'music room' working on the rap songs he was convinced would one day make him famous. And in the evenings, when he prowled the streets in his gold-coloured Nissan, taking videos of women walking along, or sitting in restaurant windows, or when he followed them home and stood outside their windows masturbating as he watched them undress, still no one ever caught him.

Over in Scarborough, where Bernardo had given his blood sample back in 1990 as part of the search for the Scarborough Rapist, the investigation was progressing with agonising slowness. The lab had finally managed to test all the samples and the list of suspects had been whittled down to just five. Now all that remained was to do a full DNA test on all five samples. However, this was time consuming, and already the specialist lab had a backlog of other cases waiting to be tested. There was no way the results would be available for another six months at least. Without knowing it, fate had just bought Paul Bernardo more time and he wasn't about to waste it...

Thursday, 16 April 1992 was the last school-day before the long Easter weekend. Like most of her classmates, 15-year-old Kristen French was in a buoyant mood as she set out on the short 15-minute walk home from school with three luxurious days ahead of her to spend relaxing around the house with her family and dog, or out somewhere with her boyfriend Elton. True, the weather could have been a little better, but when you're young and bright and popular, with the whole of life stretching out tantalisingly in front of you, and a bright, sunny future ahead, one dull drizzly day really doesn't make any odds.

When a car pulled into the car park of a church along her route, Kristen really didn't pay too much attention. The occupants, a young couple, both with blonde hair, seemed to be looking for something.

'Excuse me,' the woman called, winding down the passenger window. 'We're a bit lost. Could you help us?'

Kristen didn't think twice. From an early age, the tall slim girl with the long brown hair and ready smile had been taught to be polite and helpful. And even though everyone in the area had been watchful recently after what happened to Leslie Mahaffy, it was broad daylight on quite a busy road. Besides, everyone knew the guy who did it would turn out to be some sinister creep, nothing like this attractive, well-dressed couple, who just happened to be lost and needing some guidance.

Kristin readily crossed over to where the young woman was already getting out of the car, smiling apologetically and clutching a map in her hand.

'I'm so terrible with directions,' she said, rolling her eyes in self-mockery. 'If you could just point out the right way on the map…'

Kristen wouldn't have noticed the man get out of the driver's seat until he was right behind her, the point of his knife pressing into her side. Within seconds, she'd been bundled into the car. The only evidence she'd ever been there was a torn fragment of map and a shoe that had come loose in the brief tussle and was left behind on the car-park tarmac.

Imagine the worst fear you have for your daughter, and now multiply that by a hundred, and you still won't come near to the hell Kristen French went through over the next three days. While her distraught family made televised appeals for her safe return, just a few minutes' drive away, Kristen was fighting for her life as Paul Bernardo and Karla Homolka's sex slave.

As the video camera rolled, the terrified schoolgirl was repeatedly raped and forced to participate in twisted X-rated role-plays, all choreographed and scripted by Bernardo.

'I love you,' she was made to say again and again, just as his previous rape victims had had to do.

'You're the master. You're the most powerful man in the world.'

There was no humiliation Kristen didn't have to endure. Bernardo urinated on his victim, he attempted to defecate on her, he filmed her endlessly on the toilet, and of course he filmed her being made to have sex with Karla. In one bizarre excerpt, he taped the two women in the bathroom chatting about perfume.

'Just talk among yourselves, girls' stuff,' he demanded. As if Kristen might just be able to put aside the knowledge that she'd been abducted and was being held as a slave by a sexual sadist and his complicit wife to make small talk about scent!

But Paul Bernardo was fast losing his grip on reality. Twice over the three days, he went off in the car to get a take-out meal to bring home to his 'prize', leaving Kristen tied up in a bedroom closet. Twice, Karla had a chance to free Kristen, and twice she turned a deaf ear to the girl's desperate pleas.

That Karla Homolka was scared of her husband's violent temper is in no doubt. That she had learned how doing everything he told her without protesting was the only way to avoid being his human punchbag is also on balance of probability true. But could you, no matter how great your fear, no matter how deeply you'd been conditioned to be obedient, imagine listening to a young girl crying for her parents and not be moved to help her? Could you hear her beg for her life, knowing what hell she'd just been through and having a very good idea of what was in store for her, and not set her free?

Of course you couldn't. But Karla Homolka could. She knew she was heavily implicated in Leslie Mahaffy's death and now in Kristen French's abduction and rape. And what about the death of her own sister, Tammy? No, she simply had too much to lose to let Kristen go. And, lacking in any inbuilt moral compass, she simply didn't feel the compulsion to do the right thing that most people are guided by. Instead, in thrall to her domineering husband and shallow enough to put herself first at all times, she stood by and did nothing.

That Saturday evening, Paul went out to get Swiss-style take-out chicken. Later that night, Kristen was dead. Once again, the once golden couple would later tell wildly diverging stories about how she died. Paul would claim that he'd come back from getting the take-out to find Kristen dead, apparently having strangled herself on the cord round her neck during an altercation with Karla as she attempted to escape. Karla, meanwhile, would point the finger squarely at her husband, recalling how he'd pulled the electric cord tight around the young girl's neck later that night after yet another videotaped rape, holding it for a full seven minutes to make sure she was dead.

Whatever the truth, one fact is irrefutable. As soon as Kristen French saw Paul and Karla's faces, right at the outset in that church car park, her fate was sealed. The Bernardos knew they'd be facing life imprisonment if she was able to identify them. Kristen French would have to die. The only question was when – and how.

That Easter Sunday morning saw Paul and Karla Bernardo doing an extra zealous spring clean. Neighbours listening to them vacuuming the carpets, even in the car, approved of how nicely the couple were keeping their house. Some tenants thought that because a house was rented, you could treat it with disrespect and allow it to fall into complete disrepair, but luckily the Bernardos weren't like that.

After meticulously cleaning the house and Kristen's body, right down to chopping off her long brown hair and burning it in the fireplace in case it would show up any carpet fibres, Paul and Karla set off for lunch at her parents' house.

'It'll be a great alibi,' she assured him.

Besides, it would take her mind off the whole thing with Kristen. Over her years with Paul, Karla had become quite adept at compartmentalising her life so that when she was out with friends or family, or at work she could switch off from difficult events at home. A family meal would give her a break from having to think about the horrible thing they'd just done. For a few hours, she'd be able to be just Karla Homolka again, the cocky blonde princess who nearly always got what she wanted. In the company of her family, she could once more revert to being a child, the way she was before life got so complicated.

That night, Paul and Karla drove Kristen's body to Burlington, where Leslie Mahaffy had lived, hoping police would immediately suspect a homegrown attacker. There, at an illegal rubbish dump, they dragged the body to the top of a ditch and let it roll down, covering it loosely with leaves. Kristen French, whose life had started out with such hope and promise, ended up at the bottom of a ditch on a rubbish tip – a final, ultimate indignity.

Meanwhile, the net was starting to close in on Paul Bernardo. Despite a police error, which had the whole of Canada on alert looking for the wrong type of car they were convinced had been used in the French abduction, questions were finally starting to be asked about the fresh-faced former accountant.

One of his childhood friends, troubled by some of the remarks Paul had started to make about raping women and still struck by his resemblance to the composite picture of the Scarborough Rapist and by the coincidence that women in St Catherine's had started being raped and murdered right after Paul had moved there, had contacted the police. Within days, a couple of officers were outside his door.

Though Bernardo was nervous, this was a call he'd been expecting. And by this stage, his arrogance had grown into a deep-rooted conviction that he was above the law, so he was relaxed around the two officers – a responsible citizen with nothing to hide, but nevertheless willing to do anything to help police with their investigations into this horrendous crime.

'I already talked to the police back in Scarborough,' he told the officers, when they asked whether he'd had any previous dealings with the law. 'I guess I look a lot like the picture of the guy they put out there. I gave them some samples.'

The investigating officers were impressed. They already knew about the Scarborough connection, but the fact that Bernardo had volunteered the information so readily worked in his favour. Also in his favour was the wedding photo in pride of place, showing him and his strikingly attractive wife. Would a handsome, friendly guy like this, with a gorgeous wife and a lovely home kept so beautifully neat and tidy, really go round kidnapping and torturing young girls? It just didn't seem credible. Once again it seemed as though he was off the hook.

Despite its outwardly well-cared-for appearance, life in the Bernardo house was rapidly disintegrating, however. Karla, who'd always put her own comfort above everyone else's until she met Paul, was now locked in a battle for her very survival. Paul's violence was getting out of hand and while there was a time when his abject sorrow and tenderness afterwards had almost made up for the pain, nowadays there were few apologies. Instead, everything was her fault, everything had to be punished. Even the fact that her husband was finding it harder and harder to reach sexual climax, requiring more stimulation each time, more graphic images, more role play, more violence, was somehow her fault. She wasn't good enough for him; she wasn't sexy enough. No wonder he had to go out trawling for other women – it was all her fault!

Karla was getting beaten, but she was still no victim. There was enough of the old spirited woman left to resent what was happening and to want out. But Paul had too much over his wife for her to ever leave him. Karla Homolka, who'd got top grades throughout high school and been marked out for great things, wasn't about to end up in prison for the rest of her life. And she certainly wasn't about to risk losing the love of her family, who she increasingly saw as a safe haven from the nightmare that was the rest of her life and who, she was sure, would hate her if they ever found out what really happened to Tammy.

Paul had graduated from hitting Karla with his fists to using a flashlight, that way it didn't hurt him so much. Trouble was, it left more visible marks. One day, early in January 1993, Dorothy Homolka received an anonymous phone call at home. Later, this would transpire to be at the instigation of someone with whom Karla worked.

'You'd better get help for your daughter,' the caller said.

Arriving at the animal centre, Dorothy was horrified by what she saw. Karla had enormous, blue-black bruises on her face and one of her eyes was full of blood. Not only this, but she'd been beaten so badly around the legs that she could hardly walk.

'I was in an accident,' Karla lied to her mother. 'I'm not coming home, Mom. I can't leave Paul.'

But no caring parent could stand back and watch the life being literally beaten out of their child. The following day, the Homolkas turned up at Karla and Paul's house. Karla was there alone, in a worse physical state than she had been the day before.

'Get your things! You're coming home with us,' Karel ordered, so full of anger and contempt for Bernardo that he could hardly speak.

'I *can't*,' Karla protested weakly. 'I *can't* leave him!'

But Karel wasn't going without his daughter. While mum Dorothy and younger sister Lori gathered some of Karla's things together, Karel physically manhandled his eldest daughter towards the car. Finally she stopped resisting and, almost gratefully gave in to the inevitable.

'Fine, but just let me get something, OK?' Karla picked her way painfully back to the house, where she hobbled from room to room, clearly looking for something. Where had Paul hidden those video tapes? They had to be somewhere: the music room, maybe the roof insulation? Eventually she returned empty-handed to the car. But as they pulled away from the kerb, whatever frustration Karla felt at not being able to locate what she was looking for evaporated away. She was really leaving; she was escaping.

The house they'd moved into with such high hopes now held

so many terrifying memories, so many ghosts. In the past few weeks, she'd even started to hear voices echoing around the magnolia walls and empty, girlish footsteps padding around on the grey carpeted floors. The dead were still at large in Bayview Drive and no amount of bleaching and vacuuming could get rid of them. 'It wasn't my fault,' she'd mutter to herself in justification. 'There wasn't anything else I could have done.'

But ghosts are there to bear witness to the truth, and they always know when a person is lying.

As Karla settled back, watching the house grow smaller and smaller in the wing mirror of the car, she felt as if she'd been trapped inside one of the machines used to crush cars at the scrap-yard, but now she'd miraculously been released. Suddenly she could breathe again and the fear she'd kept bottled up inside threatening to choke her started to melt away. The nearer she got to her parents' house, the stronger she started to feel.

Of course Paul wasn't going to tell anyone anything. Why would he? He had more to lose than she did. The man who prided himself on being cleverer than anyone else, unfettered by the laws of normal men, wasn't about to let himself be shut away in a prison cell for the rest of his life.

She was still young, just 23. She could start her life over again, put the horror of the last few years behind her.

Even when her family insisted on checking Karla into hospital and filing assault charges against Paul Bernardo, she still clung to the vision of her shiny new life. With Paul banned from coming anywhere near her, she was free to go wherever she wanted. She could retrain for a new career, meet a man who'd treat her properly, have a few babies...

It never occurred to Karla that wherever you go, your ghosts come with you.

Paul was arrested on 17 February 1993 and then released back home, where he wallowed in self pity at what he saw as Karla's desertion of him. Where once he'd got his thrills making videotapes of women and girls suffering, now he threw his energies into audio tapes on which he poured out his own grief and heartbreak. Often, he threatened suicide, shrieking about the grim reaper at the door. But though the reaper knew Bayview Drive well enough by this point, it was never Bernardo he came for.

Out of hospital and living with an uncle and aunt, where Paul wouldn't find her, Karla went from strength to strength – buying new clothes and even meeting a new man she was crazy about. Life was just opening up for the former Mrs Bernardo but then the gates slammed shut again.

At the beginning of February 1993, the lab results from the Scarborough Rapist case finally came back. Of the five samples submitted, only one matched the DNA taken from the victims. The name on the sample: Paul Bernardo.

Immediately, the Bayview house was put under surveillance and police from Scarborough began talks with counterparts in St Catherine's as to whether there might be any links between earlier rapes and the more recent schoolgirl murders. While Bernardo's every move was closely monitored, officers decided it was time to have a chat to the one person who might be able to shed some light on the ex-accountant's shady past: his wife.

If there was one skill Karla Homolka had honed over the last few years, it was that of saving herself at any price. When the police turned up and asked questions about Paul's past and his sexual preferences she knew it was only a matter of time before the game was up. They'd search the house, find the videos, and unless she worked out a strategy, she'd be right up there in the dock beside her ex.

Karla had once been one of the brightest students in her class. It was about time to put those brains to use. First, she read up on everything she could about Battered Woman Syndrome – where women in abusive relationships become conditioned by sustained and habitual violence to act in ways that are completely out of character. Then she consulted a lawyer.

Karla's defence was that Paul Bernardo had controlled her by fear for so long that she had lost all free will to oppose him and had helped him fulfil his twisted fantasies because he'd threatened to kill her and her family, and later on, because he'd also threatened to reveal the truth about Tammy. She had been an unwilling victim in all of this, she asserted. He alone had carried out the murders – she had only helped him cover them up. She was willing to tell everything she knew to get Bernardo convicted in return for immunity from prosecution.

As Bernardo was arrested for his involvement in the Scarborough rapes, the authorities were negotiating over Karla's demands. Everyone knew that she was too deeply involved for blanket immunity, but if they could work out a plea where she received two lesser sentences for manslaughter of ten years each, to run concurrently, she could be out in three years or four at most. It was a pretty good deal. Even after evidence about Tammy's death accumulated, and the sentence was upped to twelve years, this was still an attractive offer. She might even be able to serve time at a provincial psychiatric hospital instead of a regulation prison. If she played her cards right and everyone bought the Battered Woman defence, Karla Homolka could be out of captivity and free to start her new life well before her thirtieth birthday.

At the beginning of May 1993, Dorothy, Karel and Lori Homolka opened a letter written by Karla and handed to them by the psychiatrist who'd been treating her.

'This is the hardest letter I've ever had to write and you'll probably all hate me once you've read it,' she began, before going on to confess that she and Paul had been responsible for Tammy's death. Paul had been in love with the younger girl and wanted to have sex with her, she told them. He had forced Karla to help him by getting and administering the drugs used to sedate her while he raped her. When she'd vomited and stopped breathing, they'd done everything they could to bring her back, but in vain.

'No words I can say can make you understand what he put me through,' lamented the ever self-serving Karla. 'I don't expect you to ever forgive me'.

Incredibly, the Homolkas did just that. Faced with the

prospect of losing another daughter, so close on losing the first, they chose instead to believe that Karla had been as much a victim as Tammy. It was Paul Bernardo who had done these terrible things. Karla, like the SS guards in the German concentration camps, had merely obeyed orders.

When details emerged of Karla Homolka's plea bargain, the Canadian public were outraged. It was a deal with the devil, they protested, not buying the whole Battered Woman thing. But the authorities persisted. Without Karla's testimony, the only evidence they had to link Paul Bernardo with the murders of Leslie Mahaffy and Kristen French was largely circumstantial, despite a thorough search of the house. Sure, they could try to get both the Bernardos convicted of murder and locked up for life, but there was always the chance that the case would collapse. They were in no doubt that Paul Bernardo was a dangerous psychopath. The only way to be sure of keeping him off the streets for ever was to give Karla a deal that would allow her back on the streets in a few years. It was, as they would repeatedly try to explain, the lesser of two evils.

At her trial in June 1993, which was subject to a blanket publicity ban, a pious-looking Karla Homolka, wearing a smart office-style suit, her long blonde hair tied demurely back, pleaded guilty to two charges of manslaughter and was sentenced to twelve years in prison.

What the authorities didn't know as they shrugged their shoulders and batted away yet another barrage of criticism was that locked away in a safe at the home of Bernardo's lawyer were six videocassettes showing the rape, torture and murder of Leslie Mahaffy and Kristen French as well as the last traumatic moments in the life of young Tammy Homolka. These tapes proved beyond doubt that Paul Bernardo had committed unspeakable crimes against these young defenceless girls; what they also proved was that Karla Homolka had played a much more active and seemingly enthusiastic part in the process than she'd previously admitted to. What was unconfirmed, however, was who had actually carried out the murders themselves.

If those tapes had been available at the time of Karla's trial, who knows how differently history might have turned out? They could have been enough to convict Paul without Karla's testimony and they would certainly have been enough to cast considerable doubt on the Battered Woman defence.

As it was, the tapes didn't surface until September of the following year after Paul Bernardo's orginal lawyer quit and his replacement, John Rosen, took over the case. Bernardo had been demanding he commit perjury by destroying the tapes and putting forward the case that he had never met either Leslie Mahaffy or Kristen French.

Bernardo's new lawyer handed the tapes in, but by then it was too late to do anything about Karla's sentence.

After his three-month trial in the summer of 1995, Paul Bernardo was found guilty of all charges, including two counts of first-degree murder. He was sentenced to life imprisonment with no possibility of parole for twenty-five years.

To this day, he languishes in an airless prison cell the size of a walk-in cupboard, locked up for twenty-three hours a day for his own protection. Gone is the cocky self-confidence, the belief that nothing can touch him; gone is the sordid secret life he hid from everyone except Karla. In his cell, with its clear glass wall facing into the prison wing, there are no secrets. Bernardo, once the pretty boy, is now pasty and out of shape, his grand plans and ambitions long forgotten in the deadening routine of daily prison life.

Karla Homolka, on the other hand, is now free. Even though the huge wave of public resentment against her after the tapes were played in court meant she served her full prison term, she was released in 2005 and is trying to build a new life for herself in Montreal under a different identity. She has even had a baby.

For the still-suffering families of Leslie Mahaffy and Kristen French, this is yet another outrage they have to deal with: Karla has her freedom, her fresh start, her future, but where was she when their daughters were begging for their own freedom, for their own futures?

Wherever she is now, Karla must be keeping her past very close to her, projecting a fresh image to the world, a blank canvas on which to draw her brand new life. And if sometimes, on the quietest nights, the ghosts still call to her, if she hears their restless footsteps padding softly through the darkest corners of her mind, well, she isn't about to complain.

Sometimes life gives you a second chance – whether or not you deserve one.

## CHAPTER 3

# ACCIDENTS DO HAPPEN

## CAROL ANN HUNTER AND ANTON LEE

Barrowgate Road, in Chiswick, West London, is the kind of place estate agents always bill as 'one of the area's premier roads'. Wide and leafy, with an eclectic mix of Edwardian terraces and large 1930s semis, its residents enjoy easy access to the River Thames to the south east and the chic restaurants and boutiques of Chiswick High Road to the north. Essentially, you have to be pretty well-heeled to live here, where properties routinely go for over a million pounds, but even among the successful, designer-clad residents, Ann Hunter stood out.

Elegant, exotic-looking, with the complexion and physique of a woman far younger than her 49 years, Ann Hunter, or Carol Ann Hunter as she was officially called, was the woman who had everything. Not only was she beautiful and wealthy, she was also one of the UK's top businesswomen. Her current job, running the

Tommee Tippee baby product empire, was just the latest in a series of high-profile managerial positions she'd held, each one more prestigious than the last. Like any successful business person, she put profit above everything, never allowing sentimentality to influence her decisions, with the result that she enjoyed a reputation for ruthless efficiency in her professional life.

On the surface, her personal life also seemed idyllic. When she wasn't enjoying the company of her two children, Ann was usually to be found with her new partner, Anton Lee, an urbane, Oxford-educated financial advisor. The two enjoyed weekend trips to European capitals, where they'd visit art galleries and eat at fine restaurants. Or they'd stay at home in the three-storey Chiswick house, companionably filling in the cryptic crossword in *The Times*.

But, as is invariably the case, not everything in Ann's life was quite as perfect as it appeared on the outside. Buried deep inside that pristine, gym-honed exterior was a parasite that was even now gnawing away at her insides, leaving behind it a trail of disease and decay, and keeping her awake at night. A woman who prided herself on her astuteness, Ann Hunter had no doubt who was responsible for this feeling of being eaten alive from the inside out. Colin Love, her ex-partner of twenty-two years, and his new wife Judy.

'I'll never be free of them,' she complained, snuggling up in Anton's arms, one night in July 2005. The two had fallen asleep after a post-dinner glass of rum. Typically, Ann had slept badly and had woken in the early hours with the usual nagging ache.

'If we didn't have children I could just cut all my losses and move on completely. But as it is, he'll always be in my life for the next twenty-five or thirty years – him and that bitch!' She spat out the last word like a bad oyster, as she always did when mentioning anything to do with Judith Crowshaw (she could never, ever think of her as Judith Love).

Anton Lee winced. Ever since he'd first started advising Ann Hunter on financial matters, he'd been completely smitten. At first, he'd been Colin's advisor, but when the couple had split up, he'd started advising Ann separately, and before long he was hopelessly and unexpectedly in love. Past 50 now, Lee had given up on meeting a woman who ticked all the right boxes – intelligent, good company, successful, attractive. As far as he was concerned, Ann Hunter was the answer to the dreams he hadn't even known he was harbouring. It was fate that they'd found each other at this stage in their lives. He knew they could be completely happy together if only she could get over this obsession with her former partner.

'He won't necessarily be around forever,' he murmured in her ear, brushing aside a lock of her long, straight black hair to nuzzle into the hollow between her shoulder and elegant neck. 'You never know, he might be in an accident. Accidents do happen, you know.'

Who was it who added the phrase: 'or can be made to happen?' Was it Hunter – raging against being replaced by a woman she considered her inferior in both looks and intellect? Or was it Lee, desperate to placate the lover he adored?

It doesn't really matter. This was a drunken conversation in the early hours of the morning, the kind lovers often have that are forgotten by the following day. And yet, somewhere within this half-whispered, half-dreamlike conversation lay the seed of a plan that would take hold in Ann Hunter's mind until it was all she could think about, a plan that would eventually bring this 'perfect' life she'd built up crashing down, burying a whole family in its ruins, as well as Lee himself – a man who loved too much.

For Colin Love, marriage to Judith Crowshaw in 2004 was a new beginning. For more than two decades, he'd been with Ann Hunter, nearly ten years his junior, ever since they were both ambitious young executives working for Avon Cosmetics. They'd gone on to have two children, but while Ann's career continued to enjoy a meteoric rise, his own reached a plateau. In their ultimate years he'd felt increasingly sidelined, remaining with the children in the couple's London home while his wife commuted to Cramlington, Northumberland, in the north-east, where her company had its headquarters. Weekends in the fifteenth-century manor house they owned in the picturesque Bedfordshire village of Wilden were frequently rushed, with Ann pulling up late on a Friday in her BMW X5 sports car, drained and exhausted. By the time she'd finally relaxed, it was time to pack up and leave again. Life seemed to be an endless round of clearing out fridges and leaving notes for the milkman, with precious little quality time together.

'It's like we're leading separate lives,' Colin, now working as a part-time business lecturer, confided in friends.

Increasingly left to his own devices in the evenings, Colin started idly perusing the Internet, looking for ways to fill his time. Like millions of others, he joined the Friends Reunited site in May 2003, hoping to reconnect with people with whom he'd lost touch in the initial single-minded phase of his career. Having spent the last thirty years making a success of his life, in mid-life he was discovering a certain hollowness that he was hoping to fill by re-establishing some of the less complicated relationships of his past. He was also curious to know what had become of some of the people he'd known in what increasingly seemed like another life altogether.

When the name Judith Crowshaw appeared on his screen, Colin Love was taken aback by the wave of emotion that engulfed him. He hadn't seen her in thirty-four years and yet the jolt of recognition brought on by the sight of her name cut through the intervening years, leaving them shredded in a pile, like so much waste paper.

Judith had been his college girlfriend when he was just 18. They'd gone out together for three years, but had lost touch completely when they split up. Now there she was again, a symbol of a different time. All he had to do was click on a key to send a message and the door to the past would magically swing open for him. It really was that easy.

After he'd sent the message, Colin was surprised at how jittery he felt.

'For goodness' sake, it's just a casual enquiry,' he told himself sternly. 'Just catching up with an old friend... She probably won't even get back to me.'

When her name flashed up in his inbox, he was again surprised to feel an intense stab of excitement. As his fingers momentarily hovered over the keyboard, he allowed himself to relish the anticipation before clicking on the message.

Anyone who has ever bought into the whole Friends Reunited phenomenon will know how rapidly adult personas painstakingly built up over years, even decades, can crumble in the face of childhood ghosts. Managing directors, judges, policemen, doctors... All become school-kids again, slotting straight back into long-forgotten classroom roles.

The last time Colin Love had seen Judith Crowshaw was when they'd been young adults with their whole lives before them, anxious not to get tied down too soon. Now they were middle-aged and wondering if life was somehow passing them by.

That first email was closely followed by many more, each one more intimate than the last. If you've ever attended a school reunion you'll know how quickly intimacy can be restored where there's a shared past. Before long, Colin, increasingly distanced from his high-flying partner Ann, was feeling a closeness that he hadn't felt with anyone else in years. Somehow those early bonds were still there, despite the passage of time. In fact, their new maturity only seemed to deepen the affection they'd put in place all those years before.

Of course circumstances could have been better. Judy was

Rebecca Harris is taken into court to stand trial for the murder of her boyfriend's wife, Jaspal Marsh (*inset*). She brutally stabbed Jaspal sixteen times during a night-time attack at the Marsh's family home. © *REX Features*

Travesty of Justice
4 Aggravated assaults
4 Forceful Confinements
2 Kidnappings
2 Brutal Murders
Karla Baby.
The Queen of Mean.
Sentenced to:
A Paltry 4 years in Jail
A fully protected
Penthouse Jail Cell
A Free University Education
IS THIS JUSTICE?

Karla Homolka and her husband Paul Bernardo – the notorious 'Ken and Barbie Killers' – kidnapped, raped and murdered young girls in Toronto, Canada, during the 1990s. One of their victims was Homolka's younger sister Tammy. Many were outraged when Karla went on to serve just twelve years in prison. *© REX Features*

Carol Ann Hunter was sentenced to eight years in prison for plotting to kill her former partner and his new wife, Judith (*inset*). © *REX Features*

Daniel and Manuela Ruda believed that the Devil had told them to murder their friend Frank Hackert. They stabbed Frank a total of sixty six times and later drank his blood.

Ian Huntley was found guilty in the now infamous case of the Soham murders. Huntley was a caretaker at school in the town. *© PA Photos*

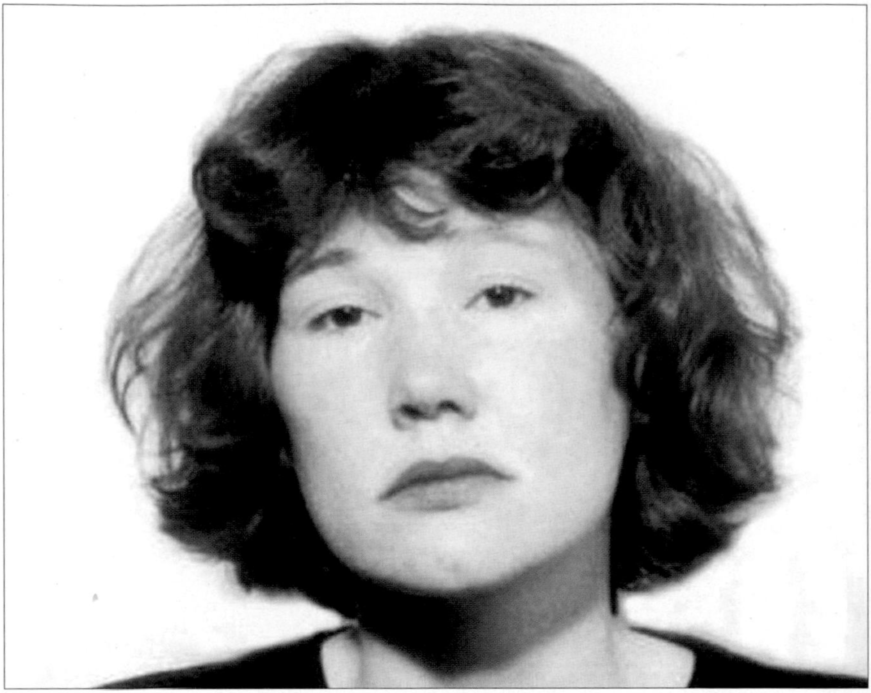

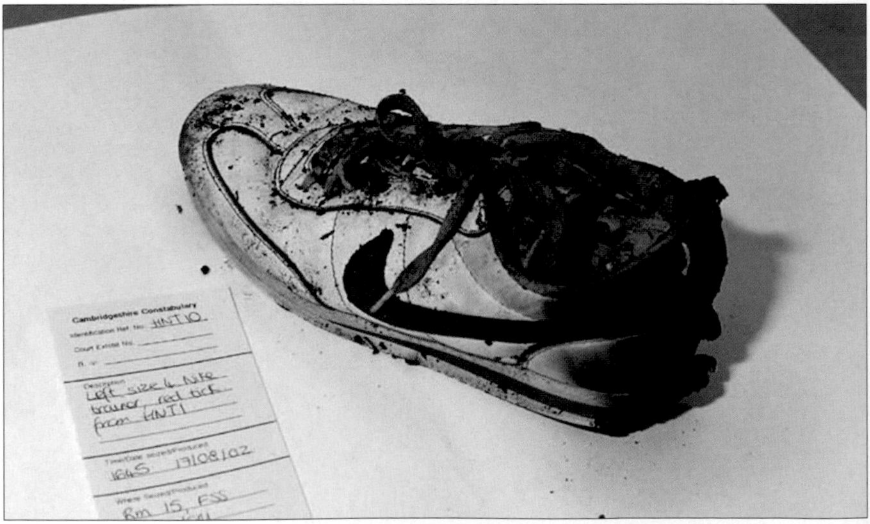


Maxine Carr, Huntley's girlfriend, lied to the police about her whereabouts on the night of the murders, to provide a vital alibi. Later, evidence, including a burnt trainer and football shirt, would help convict Huntley.

The hunt for Holly and Jessica, their fate and, later, Huntley's trial elicited strong reactions from the entire nation. *© REX Features*

Charlene and Gerald Gallego kidnapped girls throughout the 1970s, using them as their 'love slaves'. Gerald died in prison; Charlene was set free in 1997.

married, Colin all-but married. But when life throws you a wild card, an unexpected chance to change direction and start over, either you grab it with both hands or risk a lifetime of regrets.

But Ann Hunter didn't see it coming. She was not a woman used to rejection. Socially, professionally and personally, her entire life had been one seemingly effortless progression up the ladder. As the daughter of a jewellery designer mother from British Guyana and an English father who once made a living prospecting for diamonds, she had enjoyed an exotic childhood moving around the world, from South America to Europe to Africa, Australia and the Middle East. Her globetrotting background ensured she wasn't intimidated by any social or professional situation, although it also had the effect of setting her apart from everyone else. Ann Hunter was the sort of woman who tended to command respect rather than affection.

And that was always enough for her. Working until late at night during the week, and away at weekends, she simply didn't have time to cultivate close friendships or indulge in girlie nights out. Besides, she'd rather spend free time with her children Amber and Ashley, and with Colin. Why not? They had the kind of lifestyle most people can only dream of. Holidays in the Caribbean, expensive clothes… Sure, the downside was that she worked long hours, but she loved her job and knew she was good at it. As far as she was concerned, life was pretty much as good as it could be.

When asked by a local paper, interested in her top businesswoman status, what was her biggest extravagance, she cited her children and antiques. Her greatest fear was fear itself, and the answer to the question 'who or what makes you smile?', was a simple: 'My partner, Colin'. They were the responses of a successful businesswoman whose family kept her grounded – except that by the time the interview was printed in June 2005, all that had changed.

By August 2003, the relationship between Colin Love and Judith Crowshaw, which had started as an Internet correspondence between old friends, had become something much deeper. Both believed it was worth taking the chance of being together, despite the initial upheaval and unhappiness this would inevitably cause.

Ann was still an attractive woman, Colin reasoned. She'd be a great catch for anybody; she'd soon find happiness with someone else. But breaking the news was more traumatic than he could have imagined.

'You can't leave me,' Ann's voice, usually so strong and emphatic, was tremulous with shock. 'Think of everything we have together. Think of what you'd be throwing away.'

When she realised his mind was made up and there was nothing she could do about it, Ann's shock turned to outrage. She was the one who called the shots in her life, the one who was in control. How dare he turn his back on her and their perfect life together!

Ann just couldn't come to terms with the idea that Colin had found someone else. All her life, she'd got what she wanted. She'd always been the one who was chosen, the winner. It was agonisingly frustrating to discover she'd lost out in a competition she hadn't even known was taking place. Sooner or later, Ann had always known that she'd be replaced in the business world – even successful executives have a shelf life – but never, ever had she imagined that she'd be replaced in her personal life.

All the time Colin was packing his things to move full-time into the Bedfordshire house, Ann was expecting him to have second thoughts, to realise what an enormous mistake he was making. But he was not about to turn back now. It was as though a door had opened just enough to allow him a glimpse of a garden through the crack, so he couldn't go back to the way things had been: he wanted out.

Shaken, emotionally wounded, Ann brooded on the other woman who'd stolen her partner, her children's father. She'd have to be younger, was her first thought – beautiful, ambitious... In her mind, she envisaged a copy of her own youthful self. So when she discovered that her love rival was actually a personal assistant, a few years older than herself, with an ordinary, pleasant middle-aged face and a body that reflected her years, her confidence took another major blow.

It just didn't make sense to her. Ann had a personal trainer, she worked hard to maintain a physique many women half her age would envy. She was successful, well travelled, cultured... What on earth did that woman, that chubby troll, have?

The more she thought about Judith Crowshaw, the angrier she became. On the outside it was business as usual. She made the weekly trips up and down to Northumberland and kept up her rigorous regime in the gym, but inside she was seething, particularly when Judy moved into the Bedfordshire house that had always been 'their' country retreat.

When the couple first bought the house, the deal was that it would be solely in Colin's name and that he'd pay the mortgage each month, but it was Ann who paid the deposit. She'd also paid the mortgage on occasions when it had made more sense to do so. Now she couldn't bear to think of 'that woman' making herself at home in the house she'd helped to buy, sitting on furniture she'd helped to choose, cooking in the kitchen she'd helped to design.

It was a severe blow to her dignity and pride, as well as her heart. For Ann truly loved Colin, and had always imagined them growing old together. But, if she thought things were as bad as they could get, she was wrong. In 2004, Colin and Judy announced they were getting married.

Although Ann and Colin had been together twenty-two years, they'd never tied the knot. 'It doesn't make any difference once you have children,' she always told herself. 'It's just a piece of paper anyway.' Plus, with her as the major breadwinner, she didn't need the economic security that women often get from being married and knowing they'll be provided for, should the relationship fail.

But while the practical arguments for marriage had never been strong, it remained a powerful emotional statement – a symbol of commitment to one another and to a joint future. Now Colin was making that commitment to someone else.

Up until this point, Ann had been able to convince herself that Colin would soon realise he'd made a mistake. She told herself that she was still the alpha female in his life, she was the one who'd been with him for more than two decades, who'd given him children. His new love would never be able to compete with that.

Now Judith Crowshaw had something Ann had never achieved: a ring on her finger, and the legal right to be called Mrs Love. Ann had been bested by a woman she considered her inferior in every respect. It was simply intolerable.

Put yourself in Ann Hunter's designer shoes. For years she has carried around an image of herself as a super-achiever, someone who works hard to earn the successful lifestyle she enjoys, a person whose family gives her the foundations from which to soar skywards. For years she has called herself Ann Hunter-Love, convincing herself that the legal ceremony is only a formality, that she and Colin are married in every other sense of the word. And now that image is destroyed. Another woman walks around calling herself Mrs Love, only she has the certificate to prove it; another woman has taken up residence in her house, sleeping beside her man. Another woman is enjoying the fruits of her hard labour, feathering her own nest from the riches she has worked so hard to provide – a woman who is, to her uncomprehending mind, older, less attractive, less dynamic, less worthy.

Over the next few months, the natural jealousy she felt on discovering she'd been replaced in her partner's affections didn't lighten, but instead solidified into a bitterness that festered, like a tumour, inside her. Even when she started seeing Anton Lee – a great match on paper – she couldn't rid herself of the loathing that stuck like a lump in her throat. At work she was the same hard-headed businesswoman she'd always been, but at night when she was on her own, or when she was driving down the motorway to London on a Friday evening, a mist of rage and frustration and – that most unfamiliar emotion to Ann – envy, would descend, colouring everything she saw, everything she thought with a fine red tint. In bed, she'd like awake as hatred flowed like acid through her veins.

She began bombarding her former lover with abusive emails, pouring out her vitriol so it spewed like poison from Colin's inbox. He dreaded opening the messages.

'You carry the corruption and stench of the whore whenever you come down to see the children,' read one.

Judith was always portrayed as moneygrabbing, a gold-digger who exchanged sex for material gain. 'Her underhand way to get a meal ticket, by lying on her back and whispering sweet words,' spat another message, in which Judith was referred to as 'the old bitch whore (OBW)'.

Colin Love had to get used to reading about his new wife being a 'carrion crow', or 'that two-legged dog of yours'. 'The gutter is too good for her,' wrote his former lover. 'She would destroy it.'

Colin hated reading the emails, but he was also well aware of the old adage: hell hath no fury like a woman scorned. He knew he'd hurt Ann deeply, and that's why he made allowances for her bitterness, trying to allow the insults to wash over him. She'd calm down once she got used to things, he'd tell himself.

But, far from resigning herself to the new status quo, Ann Hunter was becoming more and more obsessed with the wrong that had been done to her. Soon after the horror of Colin's wedding to Judy, came a further bombshell when she discovered that if he left his estate to his new wife in his Will, she and her children would get nothing. The gorgeous, quirky old mansion where they'd all enjoyed long weekends as a family would be forever closed off to them, all the money Ann had poured into it lost. That bitch would get the lot!

That was when Ann and Anton had the conversation that they would both so greatly regret. Accidents could, and did happen, they agreed. And if they didn't, they could be made to happen.

'How would you go about it?' Ann had been trying not to ask. She'd been doing her best to put that July late-night conversation out of her head. And yet, even here on holiday in Morocco, it still kept creeping back into her mind for it seemed like a clean end to such a messy situation. She couldn't force Colin to love her again, but equally she didn't seem able to let go of him and move on with her life. The only way she could imagine breathing freely again was if something happened so that she could be sure Colin and his hateful new wife weren't together any more, living in her house, enjoying the fruits of her labour.

She wanted back the money she'd made from her investment in the Bedfordshire house, but more than that, she wanted revenge.

Anton's heart sank as Ann voiced her question. He too had been trying to get the whole conversation out of his head, to put it down to too much alcohol, or too little sleep. Now he had a double realisation: first, Ann was never going to relax until she'd got Colin and Judy out of her life for good, and second, that helping her do just that was to be his way of proving how much he loved her.

Still not quite believing what he was doing, Anton Lee set about making some enquiries. Part of him just wanted to see Ann happy, part believed hatching a plan like this would bring them closer together, and then again, he just assumed that when it came to it, they wouldn't actually go through with it. He'd do his part, but she'd change her mind at the end. They were the elite, people like him and Ann Hunter. One thing they definitely weren't were people who murdered.

'Er, Bill, it's Anton here,' Anton Lee held the receiver slightly away from his mouth, trying to hide the anxiety in his voice as he spoke to his friend William Niven. 'How do you fancy meeting up some time?'

William Niven's stint in the Army had introduced him to all sorts of people – the type you don't normally come across in everyday civilian life. People who knew how to use weapons, people who weren't afraid of physical violence, and people who could be persuaded to do anything – for a price.

While Ann enjoyed a holiday in Antigua with her children, Anton went for a pre-arranged meeting with his old friend. Even as the two men were shaking hands, he had doubts whether he could actually go through with it. Until now, this had almost been a game between himself and Ann, a secret they both shared. Was he really about to involve someone else, to make it all suddenly, horribly real?

'Erm, I was wondering...' Anton's own voice sounded suddenly strange to him, as if it was someone else's.

'You must come across all sorts of people. Do you know any ... erm ... hitmen?'

It was like something out of a low-budget TV cop show, not the kind of thing people actually said in real life. Perhaps that helped Anton distance himself from the full impact of what he was saying.

'It would need to be a professional job, something like a car crash,' he added. 'For a middle aged-couple.'

Surely anything that sounded so preposterous couldn't be taken seriously, could it? But his sweating palms and the sick feeling in his stomach told him this was far from an elaborate joke.

On his way home that night, William Niven was shaken. He couldn't believe what he'd just heard. Anton simply wasn't the kind of man to wish harm on anyone, let alone a middle-aged couple whose only crime was to fall in love. Again and again he replayed their conversation, trying to work out if he could have got it wrong. Might there have been a phrase he'd misconstrued? Could they have been talking at cross-purposes?

But then he'd remember Anton's anxious, clammy face and the way he'd been unable to meet his eyes, and he knew for sure that he hadn't misinterpreted anything. If there was one thing his spell in the military had taught him it was that a person under pressure can act in the most unexpected of ways.

Of course, that didn't help him in deciding what to do. Anton Lee was talking about committing the most terrible crime. If he was really serious, two people's lives would be over. But then again, he was a friend, and there was a certain code of honour among friends, wasn't there? In the end, he had no choice. With a heavy heart, he picked up the phone and dialled the number…

'Tell me again, I want to be sure I've got it straight,' he said.

In the hotel bed, Ann Hunter propped herself up on one elbow. The couple were enjoying a romantic night in a North London hotel to celebrate the two-year 'anti-versary' of the date Colin Love had first told Ann he was leaving her.

To besotted Anton Lee, she'd rarely looked so beautiful, her black hair swinging around her face, her brown eyes soft and huge without their customary glasses.

Once again, Anton went through the initial meeting with William Niven and how his old friend had subsequently called him to set up another meeting, with a man he knew only as 'Darren'. He was to meet Darren in a church car park to discuss what Ann wanted him to do.

'It'll cost £10,000,' Anton told her, the first time in his career in finance that he'd been faced with calculating the cost of a human life. 'But he'll do it – he'll kill them.'

By the time of the meeting, however, Ann had changed her mind. She no longer wanted Colin killed; if truth be told, she still loved her former partner and after all, he was the father of her children. Buried deep inside her was a kernel of hope that he would still, at this late stage, have a change of heart and rediscover his feelings for her. If only that overweight old whore was out of the way, he'd break free of whatever vile spell she'd cast over him and he'd come back to her! Not that she voiced these secret hopes to her current lover.

'It's just the woman she has a problem with now,' Anton explained to Darren when they met in August 2005. 'She doesn't want him killed because she doesn't want on her conscience the fact that she's got to look her kids in the eye knowing she's killed their father. And there's no point in just killing him because if you kill him everything goes to her.'

'So it's Judy who is to die.'

Once again, the whole situation was so improbable, so reminiscent of a bad TV transcript that he found it almost impossible to believe he was really sitting there, in this car park, with this total stranger. He was a professional man. All his life he'd done everything by the book – people like him just didn't arrange for other people to be murdered.

Darren, on the other hand, seemed to be taking it all in his stride.

'I'll need a description,' he said, gruffly.

Anton faltered slightly, as if realising that by describing Judith Love he was paradoxically bringing her to life, only to sign her death warrant.

'She's about 55,' he said quietly. '14 stone, with greying looks, like Dame Judi Dench.'

He fought hard to get the picture of her out of his mind,

knowing the only way he could go through with this was to objectify the intended victim, making her an obstacle that needed to be removed. Once she became a person, he'd be done for.

While he may have been battling his own doubts, when it came to what Ann wanted done, Anton Lee had no misgivings: 'She wants to kill Judith – she doesn't want Colin killed. Just take Judith out!'

As the summer of 2005 turned into autumn, sending cool breezes wafting through houses where schoolchildren in shiny shoes prepared for the winter term to start, Ann and Anton talked about little other than the 'plan'.

At one of the fancy French restaurants they loved to frequent, they looked the picture of a successful professional couple – immaculately groomed, cultivated, talking animatedly about an art exhibition they wanted to see or a polo match they'd attended. Once in the car driving home, however, their fellow diners would have been shocked at the turn their conversation took.

'I just want them both gone, out of my life!' Ann would complain, ignoring the part of her that still dreamed of reconciliation with her former partner.

Anton Lee, trained as a financial advisor to think of all the angles, tried to find another way of arriving at the outcome his lover so desperately craved.

'Is there any way you might be able to get them to move

away?' he asked. 'That way they'd sell the house and release the capital you've invested.'

If Judith died, Colin might move away, Ann conceded. He'd talked before about teaching abroad. Or, if one of them became infirm, they'd have to move out because the Bedfordshire house, hundreds of years old, was certainly not built for the disabled. That's when a second idea began to form...

By the time Ann Hunter had her first meeting with Darren in September 2005, in the gentile surroundings of Chorleywood, Hertfordshire, she'd had a change of heart about killing Judith.

It was not that she had any moral qualms she hastened to assure Darren, not wanting to appear a soft touch. After years spent honing her professional image as a tough negotiator, she knew better than to allow any hint of weakness to show through. No, her new idea was to have Judith Love beaten up so badly that she was left maimed or blinded. That would force the sale of the house as it would no longer be suitable for her, plus it would carry such ghastly memories.

'If she was damaged in such a way that it was a horrible experience, and it happened in the home, she would want to move,' Ann reasoned, as if putting forward a preferred proposal at a business meeting.

'She wouldn't necessarily have the mental aptitude to live in that home with the fear of it all happening again, particularly if he is away one or two nights a week.'

Warming to her theme, Ann expounded on her theory that a

traumatic event would force the Loves to sell up – and pay up: 'So she would put pressure on him to leave because mentally she just couldn't stand being in that home, having been duffed up so badly.'

The more she thought about this plan, the more convinced she became that it was the best option. She'd get the satisfaction of getting back the money that was rightfully hers and of knowing that the OBW was no longer living in the house that had been their family home. Plus, once she was in a wheelchair, or unable to see, Colin would doubtless grow tired of her. He wanted to be a lover, she reasoned, not a carer. To her way of thinking, it was a win-win situation.

At her second meeting with Darren, she reiterated her plan, going over the details of when and where the attack should take place.

'From my point of view, the only concern I have is that whatever you do and whichever way you do it, it looks like a break-in that's gone wrong,' she told him, unable, as usual, to resist trying to take control of the proceedings.

She emphasised the need to make sure it didn't appear that Judith Love had been deliberately targeted, to be sure that 'there is no trace back to you, and therefore no trace back to me.'

To seal their bargain, she handed over an envelope. Inside was £5,000 in cash.

'You'll get the other £5,000 when the job is done,' Ann told Darren, as if this was just one more business transaction.

If Ann Hunter was experiencing any stab of remorse for what

she was doing, if she was going through any inner turmoil at how quickly things seemed to be escalating beyond her control, she certainly didn't betray any evidence of it. After all, the first rule of business, particularly for a woman at the top, is never to get emotional.

Later, she would claim to be feeling out of her depth, desperate to stop the plan she'd set in motion with the recklessness of someone taking the handbrake off a juggernaut parked at the top of a steep hill. But, as Darren studied the inscrutable, strangely line-free face of the woman in front of him, he could detect no such reservations.

'It's all set then,' he said, expressionlessly.

Except that, luckily for Colin and Judith Love, it wasn't set at all. 'Darren' was actually an undercover police officer. When William Niven contacted the police after his initial meeting with Anton Lee, they'd set up an elaborate sting operation to catch Ann Hunter and her boyfriend red-handed. All the meetings had been taped – there really was no way out.

In October 2005 Ann Hunter and Anton Lee were arrested on charges of incitement to solicit murder and solicitation of murder respectively.

Anton Lee immediately confessed, allowing the feelings he'd been trying to keep at bay during the preceding crazy weeks to come flooding to the surface. First, was shame; deep abiding shame. All his adult life, he'd worked to make a reputation for himself as a man of integrity, at work and in private, and he'd destroyed it overnight, all out of weakness, and all for love.

But coupled with that shame was an overwhelming relief. At last the nightmare was over. Over the past few weeks, the plan that had started out as a casual, drunken conversation had opened out into a web that caught and bound him with threads of love, of passion and loyalty so intense and so twisted, it blinded him to the norms of human behaviour. It was the greatest of ironies that in trying to prove himself to Ann, he'd lost himself in the process.

Ann Hunter, however, had no such epiphany. Whenever she'd felt herself under threat in business, she'd leapt into defensive mode, and that's exactly what she did now. It had been Anton's idea, she insisted – he'd set the whole thing up. All she'd done was go along with it. She was guilty of weakness, but not malice.

At her Old Bailey trial in December 2006, she pleaded guilty to soliciting grievous bodily harm with intent against Judith Love, but not guilty to incitement to solicit murder.

'I loved Colin,' she told the court in an impassioned speech. 'I loved him like my own flesh and blood.'

She claimed to have been shocked when Anton Lee first brought up the idea of a hitman to kill either Colin or Judith or both, but to have gone along with the idea of having Judith beaten up. 'Anton knew I didn't want Judy killed in any way. But did I want her harmed? He discussed with me the various degrees of harming,' she said.

Ann, whose fearsome business reputation had been built on standing firm and having the strength of her own convictions, claimed to have been swept away by the tide of Anton Lee's

Machiavellian scheming: 'I was led into an opportunity, an opportunity I couldn't have envisaged or brought about. When that opportunity was there, I did board the plane.'

Listening to tape recordings of her meetings with Darren, she backtracked, saying she hadn't wanted to look weak in front of him and that she'd planned to cancel the hit before it was ever put into action.

But the jury didn't believe her. On 21 December 2006, she was found guilty of inciting Anton Lee to solicit murder. She had allowed her uncontrollable hatred and jealousy to overrule her common sense and now she would have to pay the price.

At the beginning of January 2007, Ann Hunter was sentenced to eight years in prison for plotting to kill her ex-partner and his wife. Anton Lee, who described himself as 'an old fool', received a four-year sentence for his part in the crime.

'It is a tragedy to see two people of ability, achievement and maturity facing sentence for such serious offences,' said the judge. 'The context of your crime is breathtaking both in its audacity and its coldness. The story seems to have touched just about every human emotion and reaction.'

When love is healthy it can set off a chain of other loving relationships. Unfortunately, the same can happen when love is diseased. Anton Lee's love for Ann Hunter was wilfully, destructively blind, while Ann Hunter's love for Colin Love was obsessive and savagely territorial.

And the next link in the chain?

Outside the courtroom, Colin and Judith Love blinked under the unwelcome glare of the television crews' lights.

'I still find it almost impossible to believe that an intelligent and gifted woman would contemplate such a plan without fully realising the downside of exposure and failure,' remarked Colin Love. 'I am completely neutral towards her now. I have no feelings for her.'

In the end, as any spurned lover knows all too well, the antithesis of love is not hate, it is indifference.

## CHAPTER 4

# 'THE DEVIL MADE US DO IT'

## DANIEL AND MANUELA RUDA

The courtroom was packed. Over a hundred journalists and photographers jostled with police, court officials, grieving family members, and as many of the curious public as could squeeze their way in. A low-level hum of background chat permeated the entire proceedings. People snuck in drinks and brought out dog-eared novels to read during the recesses, rustling in bags with furtive intensity. It was more like a theatre spectacle than a judicial process.

And the undisputed stars of the show weren't about to miss their opportunity to bask in the spotlight. In the dock, Daniel Ruda and his wife Manuela played to their audience. The two had dressed for the occasion with elaborate care and attention to detail.

Daniel, with his close cropped hair and neat goatee probably wouldn't have attracted a second glance had you walked past him in the street. True, the 26-year-old car parts salesman's dark clothes gave him a slightly sinister air, but nothing more than any of the other tens of thousands of young people in Germany who follow a certain type of music and loosely term themselves Goths. It was only when he smiled that those sitting in the front rows of the packed courtroom felt a shudder of shock and revulsion. Not just because his top side teeth were sharpened into fangs, it was more to do with the glint in his green eyes as he flicked his long tongue around his lips for the benefit of the observers. If Daniel Ruda wasn't dangerously insane, he was doing a very good impersonation.

His wife of three years, Manuela, cut a much more exotic figure. Her long jet-black hair was partially shaved at the temples to reveal tattoos of an upside-down crucifix and a target on her skull. Her eyebrows, which were completely shaved off, had been repainted with expert precision in two finely drawn black arches, perched mockingly above the dark glasses she was allowed to wear into court on account of her sensitivity to daylight. Her lips, painted deep blood-clot red, were outlined in black, like the border on a funeral invitation. Her white skin had the greyish tinge of veal kept too long and locked away in the dark. During the quieter moments in court, the hush was punctuated by the staccato of her inch-long black nails tapping impatiently on the table in front of her.

As details of their crime were revealed in court, members of the public flinched involuntarily, as if trying to shield themselves from the descriptions of the horror this couple had inflicted. Satanic worship, murder, vampirism, sixty-six separate stab wounds, and the image of a sated Manuela and Daniel, the blood of their victim, Frank Hackert, trickling from the corners of their mouths… No wonder several members of the public felt sick, while others clutched the hand of the person next to them, as if seeking comfort in the face of such inhumanity.

The only people unaffected by the sickening descriptions were the Rudas themselves. As others gasped in uncomprehending revulsion at the things they'd done, they smiled broadly, as if receiving some kind of accolade, sending one another glances of mutual congratulation and delight. During the more gruesome accounts, they kept their eyes on the Frank Hackert's parents, drinking in each new display of grief or pain, occasionally licking their lips appreciatively or making devil horn signs with their fingers.

If ever there was a couple who seemed somehow not quite human, it was Daniel and Manuela Ruda.

BLACK-HAIRED VAMPIRE SEEKS PRINCESS OF DARKNESS WHO HATES EVERYONE AND EVERYTHING AND HAS BIDDEN FAREWELL TO LIFE.

As personal ads went, this one was pretty specific and, truth be told, when Daniel Ruda placed in the classified pages of *Metal Hammer*, a black metal music fanzine, in August 2000, he wasn't really expecting to be overwhelmed with replies. Then a 23-year-old, who'd always felt detached from everyone else around him

– different and superior – he'd started to despair of ever finding someone to share his taste for the macabre and the extreme.

In marked contrast to his banal daily life selling car accessories at a parts dealer in Herten, just north of Bochum, Daniel Ruda had a deeply sinister private side. A former skinhead, he'd flirted with Nazism and Far Right politics, but always there was a voice within him urging him to go further – to be more shocking, more outrageous, to stretch the boundaries to breaking point and beyond.

Satanism gave him the extra 'edge' he was looking for. At that time in Germany, devil-worship certainly wasn't unheard of. A whole movement of disaffected young people, many from former East Germany, had turned their back on mainstream religion and begun looking at the Occult and Satanism for darker ways of expressing their disillusionment and anger. Daniel became convinced he was Satan's chosen Messenger of Death. From an early age, he shied away from human contact, flinching whenever someone tried to give him a hug or an embrace. Increasingly his thoughts turned to death and to dreams of violence and murder.

Daniel believed normal human rules and laws didn't really apply to him, that he was above them, and when he placed his lonely hearts ad, he was looking for someone equally 'special'. To his amazement, he found her.

His new soul mate was a scowling, Satan-obsessed misfit, three years his junior. Until adolescence, Manuela Ruda (née Bartel) had been an ordinary, well-adjusted middle-class girl from a small German university town called Witten in North Rhine-Westphalia, who loved animals and performed well at school. But at 13, everything changed. Manuela started experimenting with radical hair cuts and clothes chosen more for their shock value than anything else.

'Why do you have to do that to yourself?' her despairing mother would ask, as her once fresh-faced daughter painted on thick black make-up round her eyes.

At school, Manuela was increasingly ostracised. Her friends no longer knew how to approach her, and she began to keep herself to herself, even attempting suicide at 14 by taking a drugs overdose. Angry at the world, as so many teenagers are, she went on demonstration after demonstration, not caring all that much what they were about, just to have something to rebel against.

By 14, Manuela Ruda claimed to have been visited by the Devil himself. At the age of 16, she had run away to London, attracted by the lively Goth scene there, and the city's traditional tolerance of eccentrics and fashion extremists.

Camden Town in north London has always been a mecca for Goths. The grubby, litter-strewn streets have been home to several legendary clubs and shops, where young people dress uniformly in black, their pallid, sun-phobic complexions contrasting shockingly with their dyed black hair, gather to listen to the music they love in the company of like-minded peers.

As with any umbrella musical movement, Goth encompasses diverse subdivisions. Some people just like to dress up on a weekend and listen to bands that are the mainstream-end of

Gothic, while others are more hardcore and never seen without their heavy make-up and black nail varnish. In Eastern Europe, some elements of the Goth scene have been linked to Far-Right racism. Then there are the Satanists and the Vampires…

The strand of Goth music called black metal has long attracted a small, but significant fan-base, who are avowedly 'anti Christian' or who actively worship the Devil. Closely linked are the devotees who claim to be living vampires, shunning daylight, hanging out in graveyards and enjoying the taste of blood.

Manuela Ruda fitted right in.

She started working in a Gothic nightclub in trendy Islington, North London. With her uncompromising clothes and hard-line attitude, Manuela naturally gravitated towards the more extreme fringes of the scene and was soon experimenting with vampirism at the so-called 'bite parties', where willing participants tried to lick blood drawn from each other's arms.

'You can't drink from the arteries,' she would later explain to an astonished courtroom. 'No one is allowed that.'

Some no doubt saw the parties, and the regular trips to graveyards, as an extension of dressing up for Halloween – the *Rocky Horror Picture Show* brought to life - but Manuela took it all in deadly earnest.

'Dig me a grave,' she begged her companions one night, as they lurked aimlessly around a shadowy graveyard. 'I want to know what it feels like to be buried alive.'

While in the UK, the young Manuela travelled up to the Scottish Highlands, where the wild, undeveloped landscape appealed to her own sense of isolation from what was considered to be normal, civilised society. Working as a chambermaid in a hotel, she even struck up a friendship with one of Scotland's most notorious eccentrics, the so-called Leopard Man of Skye, Tom Leppard, who lives in a cave and has 99.9 per cent of his body covered with leopard-print tattoos. The Leopard Man agreed to see her after she wrote to him expressing her interest and the two maintained a sporadic correspondence after that. Clearly, whatever it was Manuela was searching for during her stay in the UK wasn't to be found within mainstream British culture.

So this then was the Manuela Ruda who returned to Germany in the late 1990s, out of synch with the majority, obsessed with death and devilry, gravitating towards the ever-more extreme fringes of society, where people boasted of having souls as black as the clothes they wore. This was the Manuela who turned the pages of a music fanzine in the summer of 1999 to find an advert that seemed to jump out from the pages into her very skin, an advert she returned to again and again until the words were imprinted on her memory: 'Black-haired Vampire seeks Princess of Darkness who hates everyone and everything and has bidden farewell to life.'

Would her story, and that of Daniel Ruda and Frank Hackert, have been different, had she not replied to the ad in the fanzine? There are moments in time when fate teeters on a pinhead, where the course of a life, of many lives, is decided in a puff of air no stronger than a sigh. If Manuela hadn't picked up that paper, if she'd decided, like so many times before, to skip through the Personals' section, convinced it could hold no interest for someone like her, if she'd ringed the ad in pen only to think better of it the following day, the future of three lives might have been unrecognisably different.

There's a certain chemistry in killing, an arrangement of elements that, mixed together, causes a particular chain of reaction. This is multiplied many times over when couples kill, where the combination of the two individuals creates the chain. If just one element, one molecule is altered, the outcome is vastly different – so many 'ifs'.

When the couple finally met up, there was an immediate attraction. Each recognised in the other the same sense of alienation coupled with the same conviction of superiority, of being special, singled out. Separately they'd been outcasts, smouldering with resentment and casting around wildly for ways of channelling their anti-social rage and hostility. Together they were a unit, bolstering each other's twisted view of the world and feeding off one another's hatred. Satanism, one of several common links that first drew them together, started to become the centrepiece around which they built up the foundations of their new joint lives. What might easily have been a passing interest if they'd remained separate now solidified into the focal point of their relationship.

The couple moved in together to an apartment in Manuela's home town of Witten. Their taste in home décor was a very long way from the IKEA style with which most of their contemporaries were furnishing their first homes. The living room was dominated by an altar made from imitation human skulls while pinned to the back of the bathroom door was a black-and-white poster of hanged women. The bedroom held the heavy oak coffin in which Manuela liked to sleep and the lighting came via specialist cemetery lights. Homebase, it was not!

As the whole world welcomed in the new millennium, Daniel and Manuela wanted no part of a shiny new future. Instead, they spiralled ever deeper into a nightmare fantasy world, where vampires stalked the night streets and the Devil called the shots.

While Daniel kept up the façade of normality, travelling to his job selling bumpers and windscreen wipers in a car parts lot, behind the closed doors of their apartment, he and his oddball new girlfriend were unravelling at a terrifying rate. Alone, they'd kept their bizarre beliefs largely to themselves, forcing them to the back of their minds, knowing others would find them incomprehensible. Together, they allowed their imaginations full rein, indulging one another in ever more extreme interpretations of the world and their own place in it. Manuela, always keen to stand out from what she regarded as the ignorant masses surrounding her, had her incisors removed and animal fangs implanted in their place to mark her out as different from the rest. Then, on 30 October 2000, in a bizarre pre-Halloween ceremony, she formally dedicated her soul to the service of Satan, vowing to accept his every word as law. While Daniel worked, during the day she stayed inside, closing the shutters against the unwelcome light and often seeking out the dark security of her coffin.

One of the ideas the couple came back to again and again as they constructed their dark fantasy world, where just one master existed and they were his messengers, was that of human sacrifice.

'We can't go to be with Satan unless we give him an offering first,' they'd tell one another, by this stage not even noticing how dangerously blurred the line between role-play and reality was becoming.

In March 2001, Daniel Ruda had what he considered to be a most exciting vision: 'I was given four numbers,' he told Manuela, agitatedly. '6,6,6,7.'

For him, there was no doubt what this vision signified. 'We'll get married on 6 June, or 6/6, and then on 6 July we'll find someone to sacrifice to Satan and then kill ourselves so that we can go to be with him always,' he said.

On 6 June 2001, Daniel and Manuela were married. The bride had dyed the front of her hair a vivid pink and tied it back in a high ponytail to reveal the shaved sides of her head. At the back, the rest of her long black hair hung darkly over her shoulders, almost obscuring the outsized tattoos on her biceps. Her eyebrows had been painted into thin, mean lines that began at the bridge of her nose and travelled up her forehead, ending high at each temple. In addition, her eyes were heavily ringed with dark make-up and several large silver rings hung from her ears, as well as from the piercing in her nose and eyebrow.

No traditional wedding dress for Manuela. Instead, she wore a black PVC bondage-style corset cut low to show off the upside-down crucifix around her neck.

Her groom was also dressed entirely in black. His head was similarly shaved at the sides, with a longer, slicked-back top section. Daniel's forehead was also adorned with two decorative vertical lines and a heavy devil's horns pendant hung about his neck.

This was literally a marriage made in Hell.

While most newlyweds throw themselves into planning for their first home, perhaps their future children, Daniel Ruda and his new bride had just one topic of conversation: their human sacrifice. Such was the level of the couple's self-delusion by this point that their discussions never touched on the 'why', only the 'who', the 'where', the 'how'. As far as they were concerned, whoever they chose was privileged beyond belief, for they would get to live with Satan. It wasn't a question of who deserved to die, but who deserved to live with the Devil, their lord.

Frank Hackert, known to most as 'Hacki', was an unlikely friend for the increasingly ostracised Rudas. A co-worker of Daniel's at the auto-parts centre, the 33-year-old was everything they weren't – warm, entertaining, popular, normal even... While they listened to the impenetrable wails of black metal music, his great love was the Beatles.

'Why do you mix with those weirdos?' people would ask him,

as he prepared to meet Daniel and Manuela for a drink or something to eat.

'I dunno. They're OK really,' he'd shrug.

The truth was that Frank was the kind of person who liked to give people the benefit of the doubt. Sure, Daniel and his wife were eccentric, but since when was being different a crime? He wouldn't have liked to spend all his spare time hanging out with them, but the odd evening didn't hurt. Didn't it take all sorts to make the world an interesting place?

He would pay very dearly for his magnanimity.

'He's perfect,' Manuela told her husband approvingly. 'He's always so funny – he'll be the perfect court jester for Satan.'

At the beginning of July 2001, Frank was pleased to be invited to a drinks party round at the Rudas' flat. He was curious to know who else would be there – Manuela and Daniel kept such strange company. At the very least the evening would not be boring. The date of the party was 6 July. The Rudas would pick Frank up and bring him to the apartment.

If Frank was surprised to find himself the only guest, he didn't show it. Daniel and Manuela were so flaky perhaps they'd forgotten to invite anyone else, or just decided to abandon the whole party idea. But, as the minutes wore on, he became increasingly uneasy.

You wouldn't expect Daniel and Manuela to live in an ordinary place, but this apartment was seriously weird. The skulls, the spooky lighting, the scalpels all over the place, not to mention the banner reading 'When Satan Lives' – all of it was deeply unnerving. And then there was the behaviour of the couple themselves. Always highly strung, tonight the pair seemed particularly manic, exchanging glances as if they were both in on some fantastic, thrilling secret. Frank shivered slightly. There was something really awry here tonight, he just couldn't put it into words.

Mercifully, he would never have to.

As he sat on the sofa in the Rudas' living room, Daniel excused himself from the room. When he returned, he had a hammer in his hand and he immediately he launched a frenzied attack on his guest, smashing him brutally about the head.

Manuela was beside herself with excitement. She'd known from the minute they got back into the flat that they weren't alone, that a force field of other entities was there in the apartment with them. When Daniel had come back into the room with the hammer, she could have sworn she'd seen his eyes glowing. He really was Satan's messenger, just as he'd told her.

Frank staggered to his feet, clutching his bleeding face. Manuela knew she had to do something. She had to demonstrate her devotion to Satan, to prove herself worthy of admittance to his inner sanctum. Spotting a knife on the windowsill, she leapt up to get it, just as a voice inside her head commanded: 'Stab him in the heart!' Manuela didn't need telling twice. Snatching up the knife, she plunged it into Hacki's body again and again and again.

Frank Hackert, the man whose only crime had been to be too

open-minded and too entertaining, was stabbed a total of sixty-six times. It wasn't just a knife that was used, but other sharp instruments such as carpet cutters and a machete. Manuela and Daniel had talked many times of being 'possessed' by the Devil himself. Now there was no doubt about it. They felt euphoric, super-human. When they grew exhausted from stabbing Hacki, they used a scalpel to carve a pentagram into his chest. Now he belonged to Satan. Where the blood flowed freely, they collected it in a bowl and each drank deeply from it. The deed was done – they were on their way.

The original plan had been for the Rudas to take their own lives immediately after the murder. They had always assumed that the killing of Hacki would be their entrance fee to the joys of Hell. Once they'd made their sacrifice, the gates would magically open to them and they'd take up their rightful places with the Devil, their master. And yet, on 6 July 2001, with the first part of the plan in place, the second failed to materialise.

After the murder, still high on the adrenaline and the conviction of being conduits for some greater power, the Rudas retired to their bedroom, where they had sex on top of the oak coffin, convinced this would be their last earthly physical encounter. Afterwards, the energy that had driven them forward all evening suddenly seemed to desert them, however.

'What do we do now?' asked Manuela, urgently, eyeing the blood spatters on the wall and the scalpel still sticking out of the congealing wounds on the grotesquely mutilated body.

Daniel shrugged miserably. Just minutes before, the certainty of imminent immortality had surged through him, creating in him a life force, an invincible superhuman energy. Now he felt sated, abandoned and defeated.

They were waiting for a sign from the Devil, but there was nothing, just the overpowering scent of incense, hanging leadenly in the blood-heavy air.

'Let's get out of here,' Daniel muttered.

Carelessly cramming their belongings in bags, the couple fled to their car. They didn't know where they were going or what they were going to do. All they knew was that they had to get away from the flat while they awaited their next instructions.

So began a bizarre impromptu road trip that saw the Rudas criss-crossing Germany, making pilgrimages to places with links to the world of Satanism they'd so whole-heartedly embraced. Sonderhausen, Apold and Jena were all towns connected with a crime, infamous in Germany, known as The Case of Satan's Children. In 1993, three schoolboys who lived near Jena and were members of the same nationalistic black metal band, Absurd, had been found guilty of the supposedly black-magic inspired killing of one of their classmates. On his release, one of the youths – Hendrik Möbus – had settled in Sondershausen, where his public neo-Nazi leanings had soon seen him back behind bars. His brother, who'd taken his place in the band, ran a black metal label in Apold. For the impressionable Rudas, these towns therefore held an almost mystical significance.

Picture Manuela and Daniel in the week following the murder as they aimlessly drifted around Germany, looking vainly for connections to the 'master' who had deserted them. They'd planned this moment for so long, convinced a ritualistic killing would become their passport to Hell, only to find themselves cast adrift and abandoned, all sense of purpose faded to nothing.

Manuela, in particular, was grief-stricken. She'd told herself that when they gave Satan their gift of Hacki's soul, she'd be turned into a vampire. Freed from the torture of everyday life among ordinary people with their drab mediocrity and uncomprehending stares, she'd commit herself to Satan's service and fully become a creature of the night.

On the day of the murder, still sure of their imminent acceptance to Satan's inner circle, the couple had written their farewell letters. It had all seemed so simple then – they'd carry out the killing, then slash their own wrists, or get hold of a gun, or smash their car headlong into an oncoming truck. But then, whatever power sustained them through their gruesome frenzied crime left just as suddenly as it had arrived. Days later, they were still driving pointlessly around, waiting to be shown what to do.

In the end it would be the laws of man, rather than those of the Devil, that would dictate the couple's next move.

Receiving what appeared to be a suicide letter from her daughter, Manuela's mother panicked. 'I am not of this world,' her daughter had written, in typical over-blown grandiose style. 'I must liberate my soul from the mortal flesh.'

Manuela's mother had long ago stopped trying to understand the girl whose every move for the past decade seemed designed to shock and horrify, but that didn't mean she didn't still care about her and worry about what happened to her.

On 9 July, with a sense of deep foreboding, Manuela's mother approached the police and accompanied them to the Rudas' apartment in Witten. The shutters were closed, and the lights didn't work, but it was immediately obvious from the dark blood spatters on the walls and the stench of decay that hung in the putrid, festering air that something terrible had taken place inside.

It didn't take long to find the decomposing body of Frank Hackert – the man who'd loved the Beatles, who'd refused to see bad in anyone – the scalpel still lodged deep in his flesh. Nearby was a handwritten list of fifteen names of potential future victims.

For the next few days, the country was on alert looking for the Rudas. With their trademark black clothes and outrageous hair and make-up, they weren't hard to find.

On 12 July, a motorist saw the couple at a petrol station near Jena in Eastern Germany. They were arrested at a police roadblock a short time later. The Devil had failed to claim his own.

The Rudas' trial in Bochum in January 2002 was one of the most sensational in recent German history. For a month, the flamboyant couple treated the courtroom like their own personal stage, striking angry poses for cameras and making devil's horn signals to the public and in particular to the family of Frank Hackert, who attended the trial in an attempt to gain some kind of understanding of the people who could murder a man they claimed to like.

From the start, the Rudas, still supremely convinced of their own uniqueness and superiority, tried to shape the proceedings to fit their own warped viewpoint. Manuela asked for the windows in the court to be blacked out. After so many years of only going out at night-time, the light hurt her eyes, her lawyer protested. Though her request was turned down, she was allowed to wear dark glasses, the black of the lenses contrasting with the chalky white of her skin.

The couple both openly mocked the parents of their victim, staring pointedly at them, occasionally flicking out their tongues to lick their lips and opening their eyes wide in manic hilarity.

Despite the gruesome evidence against them and the horrific photos produced in the courtroom showing the victim's injuries, which led the prosecutor to exclaim, 'I have never, ever, seen such a picture of cruelty and depravity!', Manuela and Daniel refused to show one iota of remorse.

'The Devil made us do it,' was their defence.

According to them, the whole trial was a farce as there was simply no case to answer. It was Satan who'd carried out the murder, not them; all they'd done was to act as instruments of his will. They were just obeying orders, they maintained.

'If I kill a person with my car and half his bloody head is left on my bumper, it's not the car that goes to jail,' Daniel explained to a shocked courtroom. 'It's the driver who is evil. I have nothing to repent because I did nothing.'

The couple's lawyers were hoping such statements would have their clients declared mentally unfit and the case would be thrown out of court, but they were to be disappointed.

On 31 January 2002, Daniel and Manuela Ruda were found guilty of a 'terrible crime' and sentenced to fifteen and thirteen years respectively, to be served in a secure psychiatric unit.

Before the couple, smiling to the last, indulged in a passionate goodbye kiss for the benefit of the cameras, the judge pronounced them 'humans, not monsters'.

'This case was not about Satanism, but about a crime committed by two people with severe disorders,' said Judge Arno Kersting-Tombroke. 'Nothing mystical or cult-like happened here, just simple, base murder.'

## CHAPTER 5

# THE LIES THAT BIND

### IAN HUNTLEY AND MAXINE CARR

'If they think I was here on my own, they'll fit me up. You know what's happened to me in the past.' Ian's voice held that familiar note of plaintive self-pity, but there was something else mixed in this time: an edge of panic, even fear.

Sitting in her mum's house in Grimsby, Maxine Carr wasn't surprised that her fiancé was nervous. Four years before he'd been accused of raping a woman and spent time in prison, nearly having a nervous breakdown. He'd only been released when CCTV footage had shown that he'd been somewhere else completely at the time, but he'd never forgotten it. Well, you wouldn't, would you? And now, with these two young girls going missing and a National Missing Persons hunt underway, he'd be the first one under suspicion if police knew he'd been home alone when the pair came past, asking about her.

'You should never have gone anyway,' he snivelled.

That was more like him. Finding a way to turn it round to be her fault, her responsibility. Just because she'd gone back to Grimsby for the weekend, leaving him alone.

But hearing the tearful appeal in his voice, she wavered. Maxine never could resist Ian when he was like this – compliant, dependent, reaching out for her reassurance, needing her love. He had been falsely accused last time, and the whole thing had caused him to have a nervous breakdown. And besides, she acknowledged guiltily, she had been a bit flirtatious last night when she was out, as he'd predicted she would be in that row they'd had on the phone just before she went.

'Don't worry, it'll sort itself out,' she relented, her voice softening.

It wasn't as if she wasn't concerned about the two 10-year-olds – of course she was. She'd helped with their class at school, for goodness' sake, and she'd even promised them they could be her bridesmaids. But she was still hopeful they'd turn up soon enough and she didn't want Ian getting into trouble in the meantime. They'd only just settled into new jobs and got their new house the way they wanted it. She didn't want anything casting a shadow over their lives in Soham, just when things were starting to go so well.

By the time Ian came to pick her up from her mum's the following morning, she'd come to a decision. 'All right, you can tell them I was at home in the bath when the girls came past,' Maxine agreed.

She usually did end up agreeing with Ian. It was the only way to ensure any degree of domestic peace; he simply couldn't stand it if you tried to argue with him. Anyway, she told herself hopefully, she was sure it would all turn out to be nothing. Sensible girls like Holly and Jessica didn't come to any great harm, not in a quiet respectable place like Soham. They'd be back, with some explanation no one had thought of yet. And if they didn't come back, a possibility she didn't even want to think about, it meant someone else had got to them after Ian had seen them off.

'It must be awful for you, knowing you were the last one to see them,' she sympathised, remembering again how he'd gone to pieces during that last run-in with the police. 'I know the girls walked away from our place alive and well. That's all that matters,' he replied.

Maxine Carr never killed anyone. And although Ian Huntley would later insist otherwise, it seems pretty certain that she had no inkling that her fiancé might have killed anyone either. But that casual decision to lie for her man, whether prompted by loyalty, fear or just a desire for an easy life, would cost the Cambridgeshire police nearly two weeks in wasted time and resources. It would cause the families of the two missing girls untold extra stress and grief, as they lingered in that agonising limbo between hope and despair. And it would cost Maxine Carr everything.

A Saturday night out in Hollywoods nightclub in Grimsby isn't an obvious venue for meeting the love of your life. Although the town itself, once the biggest fishing port in Europe, is far from the dreary backwater its name suggests, Hollywoods has a reputation for being more of a cattle market than a romantic hotspot. But from the moment she saw him across the crowded dance floor in February 1999, Maxine Carr was instinctively attracted to Ian Huntley. He had big, liquid eyes and, when she eventually got talking to him, a way of looking at her that made her feel really special.

For Maxine, that was a novelty. She'd always thought of herself as plain and uninteresting. Though doted on by her mum, she was the youngest in her family by a long way and always felt she lagged behind her older sister. When her father walked out on the family when she was just two-and-a-half years old this did nothing to increase her confidence and left her constantly seeking male approval. At school, where she was often mocked for her surname or for being overweight, Maxine had aspired to no higher aim than to blend anonymously into the background and be left alone. Not surprisingly, in her teenage years she was beset by agonising insecurities and her self-esteem was so low she used food to punish herself, starving herself until her body was as thin and brittle as the skeletons of the fish she used to fillet at the fish factory where she worked for a time.

But Ian Huntley made her feel worthy, in the beginning at least. When he talked to her, she wasn't the pinched-face nervous girl who'd worked in a variety of dead-end jobs such as gutting fish or bathing elderly people as an assistant in an old people's home. Instead, she was someone who was worth talking to, someone worth finding out more about and eventually, someone worth loving.

'I used to be in the RAF but I had to leave on account of hurting my back,' Ian told her early on, and she'd felt impressed with both his heroic past and with the quiet resignation with which he related what must have been a crushing disappointment.

Within a month, 22-year-old Maxine had moved in with her handsome new boyfriend. Like many insecure young girls unused to acting independently, she'd dreamed of a fairytale prince coming in to rescue her from a life that seemed to hold little promise. For a while Ian Huntley seemed to fit the bill. He was older than she was, more experienced and already he seemed to have done so much in his life. She was flattered by his obvious interest in her, and grateful for his attention.

By the time Maxine discovered that half of the things her new boyfriend told her, like his training to be a professional bodybuilder, were fantasies he'd invented to boost his own fragile ego and impress young women, she was already too entrenched in their relationship to get out. Very quickly the man who'd made her feel he wanted to take care of her turned into a lazy slob who wanted her to run around after him. The man who'd boasted of past achievements and future prospects couldn't be bothered to get up from the sofa and rarely held down a job for longer than a few months. But by the time all that became clear, it was already too late.

Ian Huntley was a long way from the romantic hero of Maxine's girlhood dreams. As a boy he'd got on well enough with his schoolmates, despite the nickname 'Spadehead' – given on account of his wide forehead. But he was considered a little more cocky than his limited abilities really justified. After school he too had held a string of uninspiring jobs, but unlike Maxine, he always believed those menial positions didn't work out because he was too good for them, because he was destined for higher things – he just didn't know what yet.

If he floundered in his work life, Huntley fared little better when it came to dealings with the opposite sex in which he was inclined to be oversexed and overemotional – an explosive combination. Always attracted to younger girls, probably because they were more likely to let him take control, he made a surprise marriage at the age of 21 to teenager Claire Evans. The marriage lasted less time than it took for the wedding day hangovers to wear off, and Claire rapidly found comfort in the arms of a new man: Huntley's own brother Wayne.

For Ian Huntley, who loved to be in charge and had an inflated sense of his own self-importance, this double betrayal was a bitter pill, particularly when it was compounded some time later by his brother and ex-wife getting married. Relationships were not to be trusted, that was the lesson he took away; women would let you down.

From then on, Huntley turned his attention to ever younger girls, who were easily impressed with his pleasant, if slightly doughy looks; who didn't question his more fanciful stories, or his clumsy lovemaking. The problems came when the girls were too young – Ian didn't draw the line even at 12-year-olds – or when they refused to readily acquiesce to his amorous advances. Ian Huntley wasn't someone who took kindly to either rejection or restriction. By the time he met Maxine Carr in 1999, the 25-year-old had already come to the attention of the authorities for a string of relationships involving under-age girls, and for a series of complaints against him for sexual offences. The girls involved tended to be well under the age of consent, in one case, 11. In the year and a half prior to meeting Maxine, he'd been accused of rape four times, but there'd never been enough evidence for a conviction.

He was known to be violent with girlfriends. There was talk of him kicking one pregnant girlfriend down the stairs so that she miscarried and locking another in his bedsit, starving her of food. He was a sadistic bully to those he was involved with, and according to the nine girls who came forward to lay complaints of sexual assault or rape he was even more violent to those he didn't know. One girlfriend who had gone on to have a baby by him refused to allow him anything to do with his own daughter.

Put it this way, on paper, Ian Huntley was no great catch. But love is blind, as they say, particularly when only a limited version of the truth is given. Maxine never knew about Ian's full history although she did on one occasion provide an alibi for him in another rape charge that she was completely convinced was trumped up. Content to paddle in the shallowest waters of human relationships, all Maxine knew was that a good-looking, charming man had fallen in love with her – and she wasn't about to let him go.

Because of her insecurities and emotional neediness, Maxine Carr rapidly and willingly became psychologically reliant on Ian Huntley. When he was in a good mood, she basked in his approval, and when he wasn't she tried anxiously to win him round. Of course that didn't mean she always agreed with him, they had their rows like any other couple, but arguing made her nervous out of all proportion to the seriousness of the argument and she preferred to avoid conflict whenever possible. If she was really honest with herself, she was a bit scared of Ian when he was in a bad mood. He seemed to lose all control and could flip from Mr Nice Guy to Mr Really Really Angry in seconds.

'You've got to stand up to him, Max,' her older sister Hayley would tell her. 'You let him walk all over you.'

But Maxine was in love. Ian could be so lovely to her, that's what no one else understood. Take the anorexia, for example. He was always so concerned about her being too thin, sometimes he'd beg her to eat. And when he was away from home he'd call her, often several times a day, just to remind her that it was lunch time or tea time.

'You just don't see the side of him I see,' Maxine would say. Hayley and her husband Graham tried to get along with Ian, for Maxine's sake, but it was always a strain. Around Graham, he was always defensive, particularly when he discovered they both came from the same place – Immingham, just outside Grimsby.

'He never seems to want to talk about anything connected with home,' Graham puzzled to his wife. Either Ian was extremely unfriendly, or he had something to hide. Either way, it didn't look good.

The closer Maxine and Ian became, the less time she seemed to spend with her family.

'I can't make it then, maybe the week after,' she'd say vaguely, cancelling yet another visit.

Her family had no doubts what was behind this sudden withdrawal. Since she'd been with Ian, Maxine didn't seem to have a mind of her own – she'd changed the way she dressed to please him, and now she seemed to be cutting herself off from the people who loved her. Their concerns grew after Hayley made Maxine godmother to her baby daughter and Huntley wouldn't even allow her to go to the christening, in an attempt to put some distance between Maxine and her family.

'You can't let him tell you what to do, Max,' Hayley told her angrily. 'For goodness' sake, grow a backbone!'

But Maxine was already caught up in the desperate, approval-seeking cycle that would come to characterise her life with Ian. She loved her family, but she dreaded offending her boyfriend, hated the way his face closed up against her, shutting her out, hated the way his hands balled up into fists, his knuckles white and hard like marbles. It was easier just to do things his way. Her family would always love her unconditionally, but Ian's affection fluttered like a banner in the breeze – one gust of wind and it could be gone. It was a risk she wasn't prepared to take.

The two of them, together with Ian's dog Sadie, got into a

pattern of moving frequently. They'd worked out a scam whereby Maxine could claim benefits she wasn't really entitled to, but it meant they couldn't hang about in any one place for too long. The weeks went by in a blur of unpacking in shabby bedrooms and cooking in drab beige rented kitchens. Ian briefly changed his name from Huntley to Nixon, his mother's maiden name, in a bid to further confuse the authorities. The couple told different stories to the neighbours they left behind – they'd won the Lottery, Ian had got a great new job in New York…

Like many women caught up in a relationship where power becomes interchangeable with love, Maxine quickly learned to make excuses for Ian's increasingly volatile behaviour. He was stressed, he loved her so much that it made him act crazy, she'd done something to annoy him… No wonder he sometimes lashed out in anger; no wonder, he occasionally pulled the phone out from the socket when she was talking to her friends or family; or told her they were finished and started to hurl her things out of the flat.

'It's only because I care so much,' he'd tell her, after it had all blown over, stroking her thick brown hair and caressing the angular planes of her painfully thin face. 'I've bought you an engagement ring, haven't I? That must mean something, hey?'

And she'd forget about the bruises where he'd grabbed her arm so roughly, and the harsh words that rubbed away like sandpaper at the fragile surface of her self-esteem, and how he'd looked at her as if she were nothing to him. She'd forget the warnings of her family, and the sheepish glances from neighbours who'd heard too much through the paper-thin walls. In those moments, it was just Maxine and Ian against the world – no one else mattered.

Who would have thought her loyalty would be put so brutally to the test, with such devastating results?

It was Ian, of course, who first suggested moving out of the area. His father, Kevin Huntley, was at this time working as a school caretaker in Littleport, Cambridgeshire. When the couple stayed with him for a while, Ian fell in love with the area, which boasted many airbases and appealed to his lifelong love of plane spotting. And when Kevin told his son about another junior caretaking vacancy at Soham Village College Secondary School in Soham, Cambridgeshire, Ian was convinced this was an opportunity not to be missed.

'It'd be a great new start for both of us, Max,' he had told her excitedly when he found out he'd got an interview. 'It comes with a house and everything. We could save some money to get married, maybe start a family.'

But Maxine wasn't so convinced: she'd be leaving her family, her friends. OK, she might not have seen so much of them recently, but it was enough to know they were there if she needed them. In Soham it would just be her and Ian. What if he went into one of his tempers and decided to break up with her? Who would she call? Where would she go?

But when Ian came back from the interview, he was so buoyed up by how well it had gone that she couldn't help but get swept away by his enthusiasm. 'They asked me loads of stuff about how I'd deal with the children and make sure I kept an appropriate distance from them,' he told her, his eyes shining in a way she hadn't seen for ages. 'They asked me what I'd do if one of the kids got a crush on me,' here, he smirked a little, clearly relishing the idea of himself as a school Lothario. 'I told them I'd report it to my manager straightaway. I know they were impressed – I really think this could be our chance.'

When Ian told her that the position came with a house next to the school for a peppercorn rent, Maxine's resistance melted away. This could be really good for them. She had some private concerns about whether that other business with the rape accusation might count against Ian, but when the school rang to offer him the job she realised how silly her fears had been. Of course everyone else would have known as well as she did how ridiculous that charge was. She should never have had any doubts.

And for a while after they moved to Soham in November 2001, it really did seem like this would prove to be their lucky break. Ian was earning a steady £16,000 a year, and with the rent on 5 College Close fixed at just £25 a week, they had plenty of disposable income. For the first time, Maxine was able to start fixing up the little modern house the way she wanted it, without having to worry about moving again. Always obsessively tidy, she threw herself into housework, determined this was to be the place where her new stable life began; this was going to be a proper home.

The couple loved the little town, with its quiet residential areas, where children played in the street and people smiled at you when you walked past. Ian puffed up with pride in his new position and insisted on using the title 'Residential Site Officer' rather than 'caretaker' which he felt carried less weight. For the first time he had status, he had authority. People respected him, despite the fact that he sometimes found dealing with other staff difficult and gained a reputation for getting over-emotional if he felt slighted at work.

'I'll put in a good word with you at the primary school, Max,' he told his fiancée, knowing that St Andrew's Primary, the other school that shared the same site as Soham Village College, was looking for a temporary classroom assistant.

Even though it was voluntary, Maxine felt a thrill of joy when she heard she'd got the post. It was a position of trust, working with children. They must think she was worth something. Life really did seem as if it was finally going their way.

Of course that didn't mean it was all sunshine and roses. Ian could still fly into rages for no reason whatsoever, and as for helping around the house, he probably thought the toilets cleaned themselves! God job Maxine enjoyed housework. Well, 'enjoyed' probably wasn't the word for it, she felt compelled to do it, not being able to relax until she knew there wasn't a drawer even slightly open or a surface not dusted. But on the whole, life was pretty good.

Maxine loved her new job helping with the little kids in the classroom at St Andrews. She made herself so useful that when the first temporary placement came to an end, she was given another – this time helping in one of the Year Five classes with the older kids in their penultimate year of primary school. Maxine got on well with all the children – at that age they tended to be friendly and helpful, eager to show how responsible they were. But two girls were to become particularly close to her – Holly Wells and Jessica Chapman.

Holly and Jessica were 10 years old, with shiny, neatly brushed hair and fresh, unguarded smiles. Their lives were typical of pre-pubescent girls all over the country – they hung out with their families, listened to music in their bedrooms with their friends, talked about animals, about boys in their class, about what they wanted to do when they grew up... And sometimes they talked about Maxine, their new classroom assistant. She was cool, they decided, with her fashionable clothes and her young, smiling fiancé and their lovely old dog. They'd asked if they could be bridesmaids at her wedding and had been thrilled when she told them they could.

There's something so magical about girls this age – one minute they're trying on make-up to make themselves older, the next squealing with delight over a new packet of sweets or a cute puppy glimpsed in the street. It's something about the sheer potential in their bright, clear eyes, the undimmed innocence; the unquestioning belief that life will open up before them like a delicious box of chocolates just waiting to be tasted. No wonder Maxine, with her history of neuroses and disappointments, responded to Holly and Jessica's smiling optimism. If life was such an adventure for them, why couldn't it be so for her? Why shouldn't this be the new start Ian had been promising?

But as the months wore on, the sheen started to come off the shiny new life Maxine had been hoping for. While Ian seemed to be getting on well at work, where he had won the confidence of his bosses by reporting a pupil who seemed to be getting over-close, at home he was still ordering her around and expecting her to clean up after him. Dishes he'd used remained piled up in the sink, the congealing food creating a rank fug that hung in the kitchen, until she came home to wash them up; dirty clothes were left on the floor for her to pick up. Something like her forgetting to stock up on muesli would send him into a bad mood that could last for hours.

In bed, there was little passion. Although they told everyone they were planning on starting a family, there was a distance between them that limited physical contact. Ian started chatting up one of the staff members at his school, Maxine tossed flirtatious glances at some of the customers at their favourite pub. It wasn't enough to make Maxine worried, but it did take the edge off their brave new world.

Far more immediately upsetting was when she failed to get the full-time job that she had applied for at the primary school in the summer term on 2002. She'd been so happy there, so convinced she'd made a good impression with both the staff and the children, but it had been felt that she lacked boundaries when dealing with the kids, that she allowed herself to get too involved with them. The rejection was a crushing blow for an already fragile ego.

'I worked really hard for them,' she sobbed to Ian. 'Those kids loved me!'

And Ian did his best to comfort her, revealing that often hidden side of him that made her feel they did have a future together after all, that they were in love with each other.

'You'll get another job, Max,' he told her. 'I'll help sort you out – I know loads of people now.'

That was Ian all over – wanting to help but unable to resist taking control even over her misery, wanting to be the one to supply the solution, to fix things.

On the last day of term, Maxine was again in tears as she opened the cards the children had made for her, all thanking her for looking after them and telling her how much they were going to miss her. Typically, Jessica and Holly had laboured long and hard to make their cards perfect, their rounded childish writing spelling out their hopes that she'd come back and see them soon. 'Miss u a lot. Hope to c u soon,' Holly had written in different coloured pens. The letters spilled like petals across the page.

Then came the holidays. The summer of 2002 brought the usual mixture of lazy sun-dappled afternoons, where the normally quiet streets echoed with the shrieks of children playing and long damp days where the rain-clouds hung heavy over Soham like an unfulfilled promise.

At 5 College Close, Ian and Maxine relaxed into the slower pace of summer life, but still the petty arguments continued. Not long after the start of the holidays, Maxine decided to go home to Grimsby for the weekend to see her mother. Naturally, this plunged Ian into the blackest of humours. Not only would she be spending time with her family, which always made him nervous, but also he'd be stuck at home on his own. A man of very few inner resources, Ian Huntley hated to be alone. Boredom made him frustrated and jumpy.

'It's only a few days,' Maxine told him, uncharacteristically sticking to her guns. Ian could be so controlling sometimes, she needed to get away for a while to relax among people who accepted her for who she was, without picking her up on stuff all the time. 'You can have a nice weekend just lounging about watching the football on the telly.'

But Ian Huntley soon grew bored of watching the TV after Maxine left on Saturday, 3 August. And he wasn't the kind of man who made friends easily, so he didn't have anyone to call up. Instead, he stayed in the house brooding on Maxine's 'desertion' and imagining all the things she'd be getting up to without him there to keep an eye on her. By the Sunday afternoon, he was in a terrible mood, his deep-seated jealousy and insecurities compounded by the uncustomary solitude and the patchy grey drizzle.

Around 6.25pm, he dialled Maxine's mobile number.

'I can't talk long, I'm off out with my mum later,' she told him, the physical distance between them making her unusually assertive.

'But you went out last night!'

Ian wasn't happy at all. He knew that whenever Maxine went out with her mother, she always had a few drinks and got silly. And he knew the kind of places they went to – full of men on the hunt for tipsy women who just might have checked their inhibitions in with their coats, just as he himself had been on many occasions in the past.

'I don't want you going out again,' he raged at her. 'You're just going out on the pull!'

For once Maxine held firm. Who did he think he was, trying to tell her what she could and couldn't do with her own mother? She knew there'd be a scene when she got back to Soham, but just at that moment she didn't care. She was on holiday for a few days, and she was determined to enjoy it.

It was 6.28pm when Ian Huntley came off the phone from his fiancée. He was fuming, his fingers digging painfully into the palms of his hands, his jaw clenched tightly shut… He was still seething when the phone beeped three minutes later, indicating a text. 'Don't make me feel bad that I'm with my family,' Maxine had written.

And then he saw them. Two little girls in matching Manchester United shirts, arms linked in giggling friendship, walking up the rain-darkened road towards his house, a blaze of red in the grey afternoon like wild poppies growing on a motorway embankment.

How must they have looked to Ian Huntley, the bully, who already had a long history of sexual attacks on young girls? Ian Huntley, the control freak, who had just had a row with the girlfriend he thought was behaving disrespectfully, who now needed to reassert his authority over someone else? The emotionally unstable Ian Huntley, whose unstoppable anger shot to the surface, who confused love with control and sex with power.

Did Jessica and Holly see Ian Huntley on his doorstep, washing his dog, as he claims? Did they stop to pet their pretty young teaching assistant's Alsatian and shyly ask her fiancé where she was? Did he tell them she was inside taking a bath, perhaps invite them in to wait for her? Might he have done something to one or both of them that savagely ripped the freshly scrubbed smiles from their young faces? Did he see a mist as red as their shirts descend? Perhaps he panicked, hitting out against pretty mouths now contorted in fear. Did he press his hand hard against a scream that seemed to echo the one rising up somewhere in his own gullet? Did dawning horror and reality spew up inside him so much that he threw up on the floor, where just moments before children's feet had trodden, lightly, tentatively in rubber-soled trainers?

No one knows exactly what happened to Jessica Chapman and Holly Wells once they walked through the door of 5 College Close. All we know is that when they came out again, they were being carried, slumped, lifeless. Somewhere in that house the giggling abruptly stopped and two heads, one brown, one blonde, flopped brokenly forward like puppets on cut strings.

This is the truth according to Ian Huntley, a known fantasist who lied about his RAF training, about winning the Lottery, about being a professional bodybuilder: Holly had a nosebleed, he recalled. He offers to help, leads the girls into the house and up to the bathroom. Jessica needs to use the loo, so he and Holly wait in the bedroom. A drop of blood falls from Holly's nose onto the duvet cover, red to match her shirt. She is embarrassed, fumblingly apologetic. He says it doesn't matter. Then Holly sits on the edge of a bath filled with water. He slips and she falls, bangs her head and floats under the surface, hair spreading out like a golden cloud. He needs to do something, but now Jessica is screaming, 'You pushed her, you pushed her!' Huntley can't think for the screaming, he needs to make her shut up. He presses his hand to her mouth, waiting for her to stop, knowing there's something he ought to be doing, unable to work out what. There are two girls in matching red shirts, one under the water, one on the floor. Neither is moving. He crawls onto the landing, throws up, rocks himself to and fro to the rhythm of the thought in his head that says 'No, no, no, no!'

One by now, he carries the bodies down the narrow stairs, their arms hanging limply, hair trailing. Despite being wrapped in a bin bag, Holly's wet clothes leave damp patches on his shirt. It's like being trapped in a bad dream, one you can never wake up from.

He has to bend the girls' knees to get them to fit into the boot of his red Ford Fiesta. Somehow it feels wrong to be shutting them in the dark, even though they're dead. He drives to Thetford Forest Park, Suffolk, near Lakenham air base, seventeen miles away – He's been here before, watching the planes landing and taking off, and he envies them the freedom to come and go as they please. In a ditch nearby, he unloads the girls' bodies, not looking at their faces, not wanting to make it real. He has brought scissors to cut off their clothes – shirts, tracksuit trousers, knickers, Holly's first bra, worn with such shy pride – all torn now, reduced to so many rags, which he stuffs into a bin bag. Then he fetches a petrol can from the car, sprinkles liquid into the ditch without looking too closely. It's funny the way your mind sometimes allows you to see, without really recognising what you're seeing. Huntley wears gloves – he doesn't want to leave fingerprints, doesn't want to burn his fingers. He tosses in a match and turns away, not wishing to watch the flames grow higher.

He returns home and he tells himself it hasn't happened. When villagers out searching for two missing girls ask if he has seen them, he says 'no'. Later, when he uses his keys to help a police officer look round the school grounds, he also keeps quiet about seeing the girls. It's only after the police officer leaves and two more searchers arrive, that he 'remembers' that he did see the girls after all, that they came past while he was outside washing the dog, that they asked about Maxine and that they went on their way still laughing, their high-pitched giggles hanging in the air even after they'd gone.

Of course it didn't happen the way Huntley says it did. Fit, healthy girls don't drown in a foot of bathwater or suffocate from a hand pressed to the mouth. People don't kill other people and then take extreme pains to dispose of the bodies except to cover something up, something they don't want anyone to know they've done. But in the absence of truth, the kinder lie prevails – Holly floating painlessly in the water, Jessica breathing one moment and not the next: a freak accident and an act of panic.

By the time Maxine returned to College Close on Tuesday, 6

August, everything in the house was back to normal, although she was surprised to find the duvet and its cover both sopping wet in the washing machine.

'It needed a clean,' Ian told her, not meeting her eyes.

From her phone conversations with Ian the night before, Maxine already knew that the girls had been in the house while she wasn't there, knew that one of them had been in the bedroom, and yet she didn't think, or refused to think, the worst. True, her mind skated briefly across the surface of the word 'sex' – although never in relation to the children. Had Ian had another woman in her house? Instantly she steered her thoughts away again. Ian needed her help, just as he had done before when he had been falsely accused of rape. She would not doubt him.

Outside the house, the world was anything but normal. Soham, once an active, bustling place, hung suspended in time. Its heart stopped at 6.28pm on Sunday, 4 August, when Holly Wells and Jessica Chapman disappeared off the footage of the town's CCTV cameras. Police in reflective jackets stopped cars and knocked on doors, showing the already familiar photo of two little girls in red football shirts, hoping to jog someone's memory, to dredge up a clue.

Two sets of parents, whose daughters had wandered off from a family barbecue and never came home again, waited by telephones that rang constantly but never with the voices they most wanted to hear. Where children had once played in the nondescript residential streets, now journalists and TV crews roamed around, looking for a new spin on a story that gripped the nation.

'I could have been the last friendly face those girls ever saw, Max,' Ian Huntley told his fiancée, after he got her to agree to say that she was home all along. It was a line he was to repeat to the newsmen and press reporters who called on the helpful, if slightly jobsworthy school caretaker, asking him again and again to describe how the girls had looked as they walked away laughing.

Three days after the girls went missing, at a press conference in Soham Village College, Ian Huntley spotted a tall figure, his bald head making him instantly familiar, although there were new black shadows around the eyes and his broad shoulders seemed to sag under an invisible weight. It was Kevin Wells, Holly's father. Huntley hovered uncertainly by the other man's shoulder until he gained his attention.

'I'm so sorry, Kev. I didn't know it was your daughter,' he said.

Kevin Wells, fielding questions from police, from well-wishers, from the world's press, didn't stop to consider what the nervous-looking caretaker meant by this.

'Thanks,' he told him wearily. 'It beggars belief, doesn't it?'

Maxine too found herself the focus of media attention. She'd known the girls personally; her fiancé had spoken to them just before they disappeared. Her demeanour when she was interviewed was concerned, but ever-so-slightly self-important, as if a part of her was almost enjoying the attention.

'I was inside, in the bath,' she repeated so many times she almost came to believe it herself. 'Now, of course I wish I'd been downstairs. I could have talked to them, found out where they were going, stopped them… Ian didn't know them well enough. He blames himself.'

What conversations did the couple have at night after the news reporters filed their copy and the cameramen had packed their lights and their sound equipment back into their car boots? Did they talk about the journalists, about the search? Perhaps they speculated on what had happened to the girls, on the ever-diminishing chances of them being found alive. Did Ian Huntley keep up the pretence, even behind closed doors, of being the last friendly face the girls saw, the helpful caretaker wracked with self-reproach at not having done more to stop them going off into whatever dark fate awaited them?

There are those who will always believe that Maxine Carr knew exactly what her fiancé had done in their spotlessly clean home. That she continued taking baths in the bath where she knew Holly had drowned, that she piled shopping bags into the same car boot she knew had been used to transport the girls' bodies. There are those who go further and claim that she orchestrated the disposal of the bodies, the cleaning of the house. But most people believe what the jury believed, that Maxine Carr was a woman used to deferring to her man, that she was easy to manipulate and that she believed him utterly when he said he'd waved the girls off, laughing as they went.

'They'll fit me up for this, if they can,' he'd told her, right at the start. And she believed he was right. After all, hadn't they tried to pin that other rape charge on him? But she knew Ian: she knew he wasn't capable of lying about something like this. He'd go straight to pieces. She couldn't wait for them to find out what had really happened to those girls so they could all get on with their lives.

But slowly, very slowly, evidence was coming in that would shred Maxine's certainties one by one until they floated away like dust on the Soham summer breeze. A television interview with the concerned caretaker who'd provided the last-known sighting of Holly Wells and Jessica Chapman prompted a phone call to police. It was from a woman in Grimsby whose daughter was one of those who claimed to have been sexually assaulted by Ian Huntley. Did police know the man on the TV who was talking about the disappearance of those two little girls had been investigated for rape?

Suddenly Ian Huntley was no longer a witness, but a number one suspect.

On Friday, 16 August, Ian and Maxine were questioned again at length. Again Ian told his happy-ending fairy story – the girls came skipping past when he was outside with the dog, they asked about Maxine. Then they went off 'happy as Larry'. He'd told the tale enough times he'd almost started to believe it.

Later that night, nearly two weeks after the girls disappeared, a police officer searched a storage hanger belonging to Soham Village College. It was full of stuff and he held out little hope of finding anything of interest, but he started anyway, picking his way through the contents of several large plastic bins. The third bin was lined with a black bin liner. After removing it, the policeman leaned in to look at the contents and his heart gave a sudden lurch. At the bottom was a pile of what looked to be rags. One of them was red, with black letters and part of a number visible. It was a Manchester United football shirt. The material smelled scorched, as if it had been partially burned. Holly and Jessica's clothes had been found.

Earlier that night, while Maxine went to a hotel room provided by police, Ian Huntley had gone to stay with his parents.

'I really need to talk to you about something,' he'd told his mum, Lynda Nixon, on the phone, his voice strange and strained, like an over-tightened violin string.

'No wonder he sounds so stressed,' his parents told each other. 'After all he's been through, all the questions and the interviews. You're bound to blame yourself, aren't you, if you're the last person they spoke to, you're bound to wonder if you could have done more?'

When Ian arrived at his father Kevin's house, he was in no fit state to talk about anything – exhausted, over-emotional. 'I just needed a break from everything,' he told his family, but there was no need to explain. Everyone in the country could see how things in Soham stood – the pain etched deep on a whole town's collective face.

Meanwhile, on the news, the police were digging up the garden of No. 5 College Close and questioning a couple. The Huntleys looked at one another: something was very wrong. But Ian's parents never got a chance to ask their son what was on his mind. The sky through the gap in the curtains was still black and steeped in inky night when there was an almighty crash at the front door. Before they had a chance to work out what was happening, police had stormed the house and dragged Ian from his bed.

'What's going on?' his parents repeatedly asked, their minds still wrapped in an insulating layer of sleep. 'What's happening?'

Saturday, 17 August was the day the police announced that Ian Huntley and Maxine Carr had been arrested in connection with the disappearance of Holly Wells and Jessica Chapman. Within a few hours, the word 'disappearance' had been changed to 'murder'.

It was a couple of farm workers who stumbled across the kind of discovery no one ever wants to make. The two were walking along a deserted track near a medieval church on Common Drove in Wangford Fen nature reserve just after midday on a Saturday in mid-August. Though the clouds above seemed pregnant with unshed rain, it was still the kind of day that makes walking in the English countryside a privilege. But then came the glimpse of something odd in a ditch followed by the moment of frozen disbelief, the mind's refusal to believe what the eyes are seeing: innocence lying dead and rotting among the rushes. Two small bodies, lying side by side, legs slightly bent. The arm of one slightly under that of the other, linked in death as in life.

At the police station, Maxine Carr still clung to her conviction that everything would work out in the end. 'I don't need a solicitor,' she told police. 'I haven't got anything to hide really. Nothing.' She did admit, straightaway, to having lied about being in Soham on the night the girls disappeared, however. 'Sorry if I wasted time and all that,' she said, as if apologising for turning up a couple of minutes late to a meeting. She'd only done it to protect Ian, she explained. He couldn't go through another false accusation, it wasn't fair. If people knew he'd been on his own, if people knew the girls had actually come into the house, they'd jump to all the wrong conclusions. They didn't know him as she did.

But in the end it was Maxine who didn't know her man. She wasn't aware of the string of allegations of sexual assault, she didn't know about the history of inappropriate relationships with very young girls or that Jessica and Holly hadn't skipped happily away from No. 5 College Close, as Ian had always maintained. When police told her that the girls' bodies had been found near Lakenheath air base, where Huntley used to go, and that their clothes had been found in a hangar at Ian's school and his fingerprints were on the bag the clothes were in, she still refused to accept it.

'I know Ian,' she sobbed. 'I know Ian better than you or anybody here or anybody else or even his mum! He is not a malicious person; he is not a violent person… I haven't done anything and I know Ian hasn't done anything!'

But the jury didn't agree.

At their trial in November 2003, Ian Huntley was found guilty of two charges of murder and Maxine Carr of conspiring to pervert the cause of justice. During the trial, it became obvious that Maxine had had a complete about-turn in her feelings for her former fiancé.

'I won't be held responsible for what that thing in the dock has done!' she sobbed at one stage, gesticulating at the man who'd once meant so much to her that she'd agreed to lie to the police just to save him from distress.

Ian Huntley was sentenced to life imprisonment. He remains in prison in Wakefield, where he has made several attempts on his life: in June 2003, he saved up 29 antidepressant tablets in a box of tea bags, and was found in his cell having a seizure. In September 2006 he took another drug overdose, and again in October 2007. Huntley is now rumoured to be in desperate need of a liver transplant following his overdoses. He has repeatedly expressed a wish to die rather than live out his days in prison.

Maxine Carr was released in May 2004 after serving twenty-one months of a three-and-a half-year sentence. Living under a new identity, she claims to be serving a life sentence of her own, reviled by the nation for doing nothing more than standing by her man, always having to look over her shoulder for the baying mob, the vigilantes.

'I was stupid and I lied, but I never had any idea what he had done,' she tells people. 'I just want to be left alone.'

The couple who were once on the verge of promising til death do us part are now firmly at war. Maxine can't understand why the most vicious headlines tend to be reserved for herself rather than her former lover. Huntley made a tape recording before his last suicide bid in which he blamed Maxine for masterminding the entire cover-up operation after the girls were killed.

In the case of Maxine Carr, love was blind and love was shallow. Love was manipulative and love allowed itself to be manipulated; love was self-serving and self-obsessed. And in the end, love blew itself to pieces in an explosion of bitterness and recriminations.

Holly Wells and Jessica Chapman would still be dead, with or without Maxine Carr. It was immature, controlling Ian Huntley with his penchant for under-age girls, his history of sexual attacks and his volatile, ungovernable temper who was the murderer. But it was Maxine who lied for love and, in doing so, compounded the agony of two sets of grieving parents and destroyed her own life in the process.

## CHAPTER 6

# THE PRINCESS AND THE BIT OF ROUGH

### GERALD AND CHARLENE GALLEGO

Andy Beal just didn't get it. Why were Craig and Mary Beth sitting in the back of that strange car? Most of the other students had already left the car park of the Carousel Restaurant in the Arden Fair shopping mall, where a college Founder's Day Dance had been held, tripping over crumpled ball dresses in their drunken high spirits and crushing wilted corsages underfoot. So what were Craig and Mary Beth doing hanging around in that unfamiliar big Oldsmobile which looked to have no one at the wheel?

If it had been any other couple, he might have suspected something dodgy – a drugs deal maybe. But not Craig and Mary Beth.

Every high school, every university campus, every small town has its own golden couple – the ones who sail through exams while excelling at sport and music, and somehow still manage to be popular as well. At California State University in Sacramento (CSUS) that couple was Craig Miller and Mary Beth Sowers.

Both from wealthy, respected families, Craig and Mary Beth were going places. Only 21 and 20 respectively, they'd managed to so impress the employers for whom they'd worked even while completing their degrees at CSUS that they were guaranteed high-ranking jobs when they graduated. Everyone who knew them was hoping for an invite to their wedding on the last day of the following year, New Year's Eve 1981. They were just the kind of people that you'd want to be around in the hope that some of their effortless luck might just rub off on you.

They weren't the kind of couple who'd be sitting in the back of a strange car in a near-deserted car park in the early hours of the morning.

'Hey, what's up?'

Andy opened the driver's door of the car ready to slide in and find out what was going on, but one look at the grim faces of the couple in the back seat froze the smile right on his face.

'You don't belong in this car, Andy,' Craig told him tersely.

As his friend was speaking, Andy became suddenly aware of the man in the passenger seat – dark, squat, unsmiling and at least ten years older than most of the people they knew.

Surprised and confused, Andy pulled back out of the car, but as he turned around, he found himself face to face with another stranger – this time a woman. Tiny and frail-looking, the woman nevertheless seemed possessed by a fury that belied her size.

'Get the hell away from my car!' she screeched, her delicate face contorted with anger. Then, to his astonishment, she reached up and slapped him around the face, the force of her anger causing him to stumble backwards, clutching his cheek.

Before he knew what was happening, the Oldsmobile was pulling away, the tops of Craig and Mary Beth's heads just visible over the back seat. Despite his shock, Andy was able to memorise the number plate as it sped towards the exit, fumes from its exhaust lingering momentarily in the fresh November air.

He just couldn't make sense of it. True, Craig and Mary Beth had lots of friends, but not like these two – the silent man and the woman with her flushed, outraged face. Who were these strange people who'd just driven off with his friends? Should he call the police, or would that just cause problems for Craig and Mary Beth, who'd clearly not wanted him to know what was going on?

Still unable to decide what to do, Andy went home but when he returned to the car park after a few sleepless hours and found Mary Beth's car still parked there, eerie in its solitude, he knew he had to report it. Little did he know when he made that call how many more sleepless nights were to come. Nights when he'd lie in bed going over and over what happened, seeing once again the man's bulky presence, the woman's face, screwed-up in anger. Nights when he'd wish again he'd done something, said something… Because the two strangers Andy Beal had just encountered in the shopping mall were Charlene and Gerald Gallego, who would soon become infamous as the Sex-Slave Murderers.

Craig and Mary Beth, the golden couple whose dazzling future shone bright and vivid in their intelligent, attractive faces, would be their latest victims.

Charlene Williams shot another furtive glance over at the man playing poker in the card-room adjoining the shabby cocktail bar where she sat. He was not handsome, that was for sure. Broad and stocky, with a barrel chest that seemed, when he stood up to go to the bathroom, too bulky to be supported by his short jeans-clad legs, he was not exactly leading man material. But there was something about his rugged features, something about the way his macho-man long dark sideburns contrasted with his big puppy-dog eyes that drew her to him.

She liked the way he swaggered when he walked, as if he owned the place. Also, how he sat at the table, a man among men, knowing she was looking his way but letting her sweat it out.

Charlene nudged the friend she was with.

'What do you think?' she asked, giggling.

Her companion looked over at the coarse little man with his greasy black hair and rough-looking companions then back at the petite and innocent-looking, well-spoken Charlene, who looked to be at least a decade his junior. Really, Charlene did have some strange taste in men! But then, despite her little-girl looks, she was a big girl of 21 now, already with two failed marriages under her slim-line belt.

'Go for it,' she shrugged.

Gerald Gallego proved every bit as unlikely a choice for Charlene Williams as he'd first appeared. Like her, he'd already been married before – six times to be exact – but there the similarities ended.

Charlene was an only child from a loving, upwardly middle-class Californian family. Her father, Charles, was a supermarket executive and her doting parents showered their little princess with time and attention, encouraging her with her school work and all the other extra-curricular activities well-off children in Arden Park, Sacramento took for granted. As a result, Charlene grew up self-assured and confident. She was also extremely bright and a precociously talented violin player.

Her father, to whom she was exceptionally close, delighted in introducing his pretty, intelligent daughter to his friends and colleagues, and she in turn adored her strong-willed charismatic Daddy. It would take an exceptionally large character to step into those smartly polished shoes.

Neither of her two husbands remotely fitted the bill. By the time she married the first at 18, Charlene had strayed considerably from the path her ambitious parents had imagined for her. Like many middle-class Californian teenagers with an instinct to rebel but nothing to rebel against, she'd settled instead for self-sabotage, replacing her earlier academic and musical promise with an equal talent for drugs and casual sex. Both her short-lived early marriages were a result of that rebellious instinct for immediate gratification, but in each Charlene quickly discovered that neither lived up to her ideal of a real man. Gerald Gallego, however, was different.

Gerald Gallego was the kind of man Charlene's parents warned her against when she was younger. His father had been executed in Mississippi for killing two policemen when Gerald was just a boy, a crime for which he declared he felt 'no regret or sorrow whatsoever'. His mother had dabbled in prostitution, and the young Gerald had grown up believing that sex was pretty much inseparable from power. As a young child, he was always in trouble, sometimes for thieving, others for sexual aggression. By the time he was 13, he'd been arrested for having sex with a 6-year-old girl.

'Bad blood will out,' people would whisper.

When he met Charlene in 1977, Gerald was 32 years old and he'd already served time in jail, been arrested at least 23 times as well as married 6 times and rarely managed to hold down a job for more than a few months at a time. He was certainly no catch, and yet, something in the loud, cocky, chauvinistic poker player appealed to Charlene. Maybe she thought that, like her father, here at last was someone to look up to, a man's man who'd be strong enough to take care of her.

For his part, Gerald Gallego was equally taken with the petite blonde who kept catching his eye across the seedy poker bar. On closer examination, he'd find her to be older than he'd originally thought, but at first glance, Charlene Williams, barely five feet tall with a tiny un-womanly frame, looked like a young schoolgirl. Which was just the type that Gerald Gallego liked.

'You're a real sweet girl,' he told her, the second time they met for a date.

'And you're a nice guy,' she replied, gazing up at him from beneath her floppy blonde hair.

Both would be proved wrong.

Within weeks of their first meeting, Charlene and Gerald were living together. At first it was exciting for Gerald was dynamic and highly sexed – he reminded her of a young Marlon Brando in *A Streetcar Named Desire*, all unarticulated passion and clumsy but overpowering sexuality. She didn't even mind the fact that he expected her to support him – Charlene had grown up in a household with a healthy respect for hard work and for the advantages it brings. She was proud of the fact that she found it easy to find, and keep, reasonably well-paid jobs. This was something Gerald couldn't compete with, and it made her feel good to see the grudging respect in his eyes when she handed over her pay packet, and to feel like he needed her.

However, the honeymoon period didn't last long.

'You're not doing it right,' Gerald would snap at her, lying rigid on his back, his flaccid penis limp against his leg like a used sponge. 'If you were a proper woman you could satisfy me. This is all your fault!'

Charlene, dressed up as per orders in a short schoolgirl's skirt and long socks, would break off from her exertions, almost crying with frustration.

'I'm doing just what you told me, Gerry,' she'd plead, feeling suddenly silly with her hair in bunches just like a 10-year-old.

She couldn't understand how the sex, which had started off so good, could have deteriorated so quickly.

'It's no good,' Gerald would rage. 'I need something different.'

Then he'd be off on his recurring fantasy, the one he came back to again and again.

'What I need is a couple of young girls I can keep as sex slaves and force to do whatever I want,' he'd start, his erection slowly stirring into life as he detailed his desires in which violence always shared equal stage with violation. Charlene was willing to do whatever he wanted in bed, but that was part of the problem – she was *too* willing. What he needed was to see fear in a girl's eyes, to feel the thrill of power as he forced her, resisting all the way, to do his bidding.

And Charlene would lie there and listen, glad to join in with anything that got him going sexually, using the imagination that had so impressed her English teachers to come up with warped suggestions of her own.

'That sounds like fun, Gerry,' she'd tell him, approvingly, watching his erection return.

What she didn't know at the beginning was that the sex slave fantasy wasn't just a figment of Gerald Gallego's twisted imagination, something he dredged up to revive a flagging sex life, but a very real plan, and one that he would expect his pretty young girlfriend to help him put into action.

It was the summer of 1978 when Gerald decided it was time to stop daydreaming and start acting. The Sacramento apartment he shared with Charlene was hot and cramped and the sweat-soaked nights made him irritable and aggressive.

Up until now it was Charlene who'd borne the brunt of his over-heated moodiness, and she still bore the bruises of times he'd lashed out at her in frustration and over-heated ill temper. But now he had new victims in mind – cool, fresh, unsullied young girls who'd quiver with terror and make him feel virile, potent and in control.

As Gerald described his plan, Charlene felt sickened and enthralled in equal measure. On the one hand, the middle-class little girl she'd once been recoiled from the savagery of it, the sheer sadism of getting pleasure through other people's pain. But on the other, she recognised that this was just an extension of the very thing that had drawn her to Gerry in the first place – his wild untamed character, his disregard for the law. Ever since adolescence, she'd wanted a bad boy. Well, now she'd found one.

'Want to come and smoke a bit of pot with me?'

Charlene had been chatting to the two pretty long-haired teenagers for quite a while before she casually tossed the invitation into the conversation.

Rhonda Scheffler, 17, glanced over at her 16-year-old friend Kippi Vaught, and saw she was already smiling. Shopping was only really fun if you had loads of money, which they didn't. The idea of escaping the crowded mall for a few moments to relax and get high with their new friend seemed pretty appealing.

Neither of them was naïve; they'd never have dreamed of going off somewhere with a strange man they'd only just met, but the blonde woman who'd approached them a few moments before was so friendly, and so young-looking – hardly older than them – they didn't have any qualms about following her outside the Country Club Plaza mall to where she said her van was parked. After all, she was so tiny it seemed as though one little gust of California wind would have blown her clean away. But it was 11 September and summer was still clinging determinedly on, so of course there was no wind, just the scorching Californian sun, beating down on the tarmac and reflecting like white heat off the car bonnets.

Approaching the van, with its distinctive air-brushed exterior depicting a futuristic landscape of sinister twisting hills, one topped with a hunch-backed vulture, Charlene began to talk loudly and quickly.

'Just a tiny bit further, girls... Here, this is it.'

Gerald, waiting inside, heard their voices and felt a current of adrenaline rush through him. This was it: this was the day all his fantasies were going to come true.

Relaxed and unwary, the girls didn't stand a chance. No sooner were they through the van door than Gerald was on them, brandishing a gun, binding their wrists and ankles with tape.

'You watch them,' he ordered Charlene, jumping behind the wheel.

As the van pulled out of the car park, Charlene perched on the ice-box in the back of the van, ignoring the girls' faces down on the floor, their eyes gazing up at her in mute, terrified appeal. Instead, she concentrated on the scenery out the window, the shopping mall receding into the distance through the back window, shimmering in the heat haze like a dream, an illusion – as unreal as the kidnapping they'd just carried out. And now she could see oak trees through the window as the van left urban Sacramento behind, heading for the foothills of the Sierra Nevada mountains, which wore their pine forests like a patchwork cloak. A person could easily get lost among the folds, absorbed into the dense stillness, shivering in the sudden shadows…

In a deserted forest clearing, Gerald finally stopped the van.

'You stay here,' he told Charlene gruffly, hardly able to speak for the power-lust that coursed through his body like larva, cutting off all messages to his brain so that the only thing that remained was his overwhelming need to degrade, to debase, to twist, to force, to own, to destroy.

Grabbing a sleeping bag, he untied the tape from the girls' ankles so that they could walk and forced them from the van at gun-point.

'Over there,' he ordered, pointing into the shadows, where the pine trees formed a natural canopy, heavy and dark as the lid of a coffin. Whimpering softly, the girls did as they were told – two young women full of promise, heading on legs that quaked and shook into the living nightmare of one man's perverted desires.

But Charlene didn't want to be left out. If this was Gerald's fantasy, she wanted to be part of it. Joining the figures under the trees, she stripped off her own clothes and showed Gerald just how much she'd learned from him. Years after giving up on school, she was once again eager to prove just how enthusiastic a student she could be.

Later, Gerald had Charlene drive home to give herself an alibi and return at midnight to pick them up in her own car, a silver-blue Oldsmobile.

And what did she think as she put her dainty foot down on the accelerator and pulled away into the darkness? Had she spared a thought for what would happen to the two girls who'd given her their trust, whose handbags lay abandoned on the floor of the van? Did she wonder what had become of the girl she'd once been, who'd worked hard and practised the violin and dreamed of a future where the world opened up to her like a flower? Or was she conditioned by now to think only of satisfying her man's desires, so bound up with her own, and content to just let reality trickle over her gently like a stream that barely registered?

By the time she returned, Gerald had finished with the girls and was ready to discard them. The car hadn't gone far when he ordered Charlene to pull over into a field stretching endlessly into the darkness.

'Turn the music up,' he commanded her. 'Loud!'

Then he yanked the girls out, and, one by one, took them off into the black night. Charlene tried not to notice the way the moonlight reflected off the gun in Gerald's hand as he disappeared into the shadows, did her best not to think of the noises and flashes in the distance, or what it meant when he returned to the car alone. He was her man: he was a man's man, he was taking care of things and he'd take care of her.

Later that night, when Gerry held her and whispered how wonderful she was, how special, Charlene told herself that it had all been worth it. He'd lived his fantasy now and she'd not only made it possible, but also made herself part of it. She'd proved herself to him and now he'd realise just how much she meant to him. From this day forth they were bound together and there was nothing either of them could do about it.

When Gerald and Charlene were married in Reno, Nevada, on 30 September 1978 it wasn't the happy occasion it should have been for the blushing bride. For a start, memories of the two girls kept popping into her mind. Then there were the child molestation charges.

Just a few days before, the couple had learned that Gerald's daughter from one of his earlier marriages had gone to the police to accuse him of sex abuse. According to the 14-year-old, her father had been sexually assaulting her on a regular basis for the past eight years.

'I haven't done anything wrong. I love that girl!' Gerry raged.

Charlene thought of the schoolgirl skirts he liked her to wear, and how he wanted her to put her hair into bunches, but she said nothing. She was fast learning that, when it came to her unpredictable boyfriend, silence was often the best policy.

The result of the charges was that Gerald decided they had to get out of California for a while. Houston, Texas sounded a good option. Charlene's father said he'd pull some favours to find Gerald a job down there, and they liked the idea of putting some distance between themselves and what had just happened over the last few weeks.

On the way, they stopped off in Reno to get married. Neither of them voiced the thought that kept going round inside their heads: A wife can't testify against her husband.

'Happy?' Gerry asked Charlene, outside the Reno courthouse. She nodded, resting her blonde head briefly on his broad shoulder. Inside she wasn't so sure. She knew she loved her new husband, and she was more excited by him than any other man she'd ever known. Her fate was tied up in his – but happy? She didn't know if she remembered what it was like to be happy.

In Houston, Gerald acquired a new identity to go with his new life: from a stolen birth certificate in the name of Stephen Feil. But Texas life didn't suit them. Gerry didn't settle in and constantly fought with the other staff at the bar where he was working, so pretty soon he and Charlene were back in Reno, where once again Charlene supported them with a well-paid job while Gerry lay about in their apartment, alone with his memories and his fantasies. With sex between the couple again once again unsatisfying and Gerald's impotence returning, it became only a matter of time before his thoughts once again turned to kidnap, rape and murder.

At Washoe County Fair, 14-year-old Brenda Judd and 13-year-old Sandra Colley were just heading off to the exit where they were supposed to be met by one of their older sisters when they bumped into Charlene. It was 24 June 1979 and the petite blonde looked hot and bothered.

'Wanna help me deliver some leaflets?' she asked, in a voice that carried a weary hint of previous refusals. 'There'll be some money in it for you.'

The girls nodded. Why not? After all they'd spent so far today, they might as well make a little bit back.

'Great! Come with me to my van and we'll pick up the leaflets,' Charlene explained.

But there were no leaflets – just Gerald, with his gun and his tape, and a thin mattress on the floor that seemed somehow more terrifying even than the weapon pointed in their faces.

This time Charlene drove, feeling that same mixture of excitement and sick dread as she listened to the sounds coming from the back of the van. They coasted out into the countryside beyond Washoe County, where a person can pitch a tent for days and not see anyone else, where the two girls were marched away from a van into a darkness that swallowed them whole.

And now there were two secrets binding the couple intrinsically together, four ghosts weaving between them a web of suspicion and fear.

'I love you, Baby,' Gerry told her and she felt like a star pupil who'd made the teacher proud – but at what cost?

Now Gerald Gallego had killed four times, and he had also got away with it four times. He'd abused his own daughter for eight years, and still he was walking around free. No wonder he started to believe he was above the law. Gratification was the name of the game, he told himself. This was a dog-eat-dog world and if a few little girls had to die to keep him happy, well, that was just the way it was. If there was one lesson life had taught this son of a murderer and a prostitute, it was that if something's worth having, it's worth taking by force.

24 April 1980 saw Gerald waking up in what he'd begun to call 'one of those moods'. He'd been building up to it for days, spending hours brooding on his own, lost in who knows what dark reveries where he relived everything he'd done, everything he'd made those girls do. Now he was like a heroin addict in need of a fix.

'Come on, Baby. One more time,' he wheedled to his wife, as though he was asking her to go and sit through a movie she'd seen before and hadn't enjoyed.

What was Charlene to do? She looked at the powerful body, capable of inflicting such pain; she looked at the gun he carried around with him like a lucky talisman, at those puppy dog eyes she'd fallen in love with just two short years before.

'I'll get my purse,' she said.

Stacy Ann Redican and Karen Twiggs had had enough of shopping. The Sunrise Mall in Citrus Heights, just outside of Sacramento was OK as shopping centres go, but there comes a time when you've just had it with trailing around store after store looking at the same old things. The two 17-year-olds were due for a break. And then they met Charlene Gallego.

'I've got my van just outside,' she told them, after they'd all got chatting outside a shop. 'Fancy going for a ride and maybe having a joint?'

They didn't need asking twice. But they didn't see Gerry, with his by now familiar kidnapping kit until it was too late…

Suddenly the van was moving and the tiny blonde girl-woman who'd been so friendly in the mall wasn't meeting their eyes and they prayed for this not to be what it seemed. And then they were face down on the stinking mattress in the back of the van and the man with the gun was telling them to take off their clothes. After that, they just prayed for oblivion.

At Limerick Canyon near Lovelock, they got their wish. One at a time, Gerald Gallego walked them off into the countryside, like a courteous suitor seeing his dates home. Each time he returned to the van alone.

By now it was like a drug – the rape, the terror, the killing. No sooner had Gerry disposed of the evidence from one attack than he was getting jittery, wanting to do another.

Gerald and Charlene were supposed to be having a mini vacation in Oregon when he spotted his next victim. Even though the woman was heavily pregnant and older than his chosen type, even though she was walking along a busy road in the middle of the day when anyone could have seen them, as soon as Gerry saw Linda Aguilar, he wanted her.

It was 7 June 1980, just weeks after the deaths of Stacy and Karen. Charlene, who'd recently discovered that she too was expecting a baby, had thought her husband would be content to lie low for a while but now she realised, and not for the first time, that she'd misjudged her bad boy.

'I want her!' Gerry announced suddenly when they'd almost passed seven months' pregnant Linda by the side of the road. 'I'm pulling over.'

Linda didn't have time to think before he'd wound the window down.

'Need a lift?' he called, with his cheeriest rogue smile. Linda looked from the grinning man behind the wheel to the woman sitting next to him, whose blonde hair seemed to reflect the sunshine right back out of the van.

'Sure,' she replied.

When they pulled up in the countryside some time later, Linda was to find her pregnancy won her little sympathy from her sex-obsessed captors. Power was the name of the game with Gerald and Charlene, and if the victim was more defenceless because of being young or heavily pregnant, well, that just added to their excitement.

When it was over, Linda, like her predecessors who'd had the misfortune to lie on that same stained and stinking mattress, was taken off and killed. By this stage Gerald had dispensed with the gun and was carrying out his murders by hitting his victims over the head with a rock or a hammer and then strangling them. He didn't mind the extra manual labour – knowing he had someone's life literally in his hands increased his feelings of power. He was in control, Gerald Gallego: he was the man.

By now Gerald had killed seven girls and Charlene, at first an enthusiastic participant in his warped fantasy, was waking up to two pretty unpleasant facts – first, he wasn't going to stop any time soon and second, she could be the next at any moment.

Even though there were times when Gerry still told her he loved her, he was also likely to beat her up the next minute, so she could never be completely certain how she stood. He may not have had the educational advantages she'd had, but even he could work out that now Charlene knew a little too much about him and what he'd done than was altogether comfortable.

Charlene Gallego, daughter of a master-strategist who'd pulled himself up from butcher to supermarket executive, was nothing if not pragmatic. It was a pity all those girls had died, but really it hadn't been her fault. She'd done what she'd had to out of fear of Gerry and because she felt a kind of duty to keep him sexually satisfied. She'd chosen him for his raw sexuality – surely she couldn't try and stop him expressing it now?

Back in California, as the rest of the world drew their blinds against the relentless sun and stayed indoors with the air con on full, leaving the outside world free for overheating tourists and panting dogs lying in the shade of the palm trees, Charlene continued to make excuses to herself. Meanwhile, the monster that lived inside her new husband grew ever fatter and more hungry to be fed.

'This is damned useless!'

Gerald, whose attention span rarely lasted longer than the average TV advertisement, was already fed up. For what seemed to him ages, he and Charlene had been fishing on the banks of the Sacramento River, but they hadn't caught much of anything. Instead they'd got steadily drunker, swigging vodka out of plastic cups as the blood-orange sun sank lower in the sky. It was 16 July 1980 and the heat of the summer seemed to mingle with the alcohol, warm and heavy through their veins.

'Let's go and get a drink.'

Of course it was futile for her to say that they'd already had far too many drinks than were good either for a pregnant woman or for someone about to get in a van and drive. Instead, Charlene packed up the fishing gear.

It was getting dark anyway, and it might be nice to find a quiet little bar some place where they could talk – Gerry had been in an uncharacteristically affectionate mood earlier, telling her how pretty she was, how lucky he was to have her. Aware of how his moods could switch more quickly than the flick of an iguana's tail, Charlene was keen to take advantage of his rare good humour. Despite everything that had happened – the murders, the fact she knew he was seeing at least one other woman, the way he lashed out at her in one of his blind rages – Gerald Gallego could still make her feel weak at the knees. One look from those big wide eyes of his and she felt her insides soften like butter in the sun. She was still his baby, she was still his number one girl. All she had to do was keep quiet and carry on helping him out.

'This place looks all right,' Gerry gestured to a cosy-looking bar with a sign outside that read The Sail Inn.

Inside the Gallegos chatted a bit with the bartenders and a group of guys who'd also spent the afternoon fishing. The drinks flowed freely and Charlene felt a warm glow. Maybe it would be all right after all. Perhaps the baby would turn them back into a normal couple with nothing more pressing on their minds than worrying about how to pay the rent.

As the lone remaining barmaid got ready to close up the bar, the Gallegos stumbled out into the car park, Charlene giggling slightly and clutching onto Gerry's arm for support. Then all of a sudden Gerald stopped walking.

'What about the barmaid?' he asked hoarsely.

Charlene didn't need to ask him what he meant. His whole body had gone tense, and even without looking at his face, she knew he'd be wearing that dark, closed look.

'No, honey,' she told him, trying to drag him over to the van. 'Lots of people saw us talking to her in there. Let's get home.'

But as they were driving out of the car park, they saw the barmaid, Virginia Mochel, getting into her own car, ready to go home after her long shift. For Gerald, this was too much temptation.

'Hey, what are you doing? Don't be crazy!' – but Charlene's protestations fell on deaf ears as her husband swung the van over to Virginia's car. Seconds later he'd pulled the stunned woman out of her car at gun point and was ushering her into the back of the van.

Charlene was expecting them to go out into the countryside as usual but this time Gerry headed the van in the direction of their apartment.

'It's too risky,' Charlene warned.

But Gerald had an image in mind. He and Charlene and their terrified prisoner on their own bed, with their own 'play things' – the dildos and whips they used in their own sex games. And the best thing was, in the privacy of their own home there were no time limits. They could extend the fantasy all night if they wanted. Which is exactly what they did.

'Why don't you kill me now?'

The Virginia Mochel lying on the couple's mattress as the first signs of light began to filter through the drawn blinds was a long way from the cheery blonde waitress they'd met at The Sail Inn just a few hours before. Gone was the welcoming smile, gone the shiny, well-brushed hair and the frank, friendly gaze. Now Virginia's eyes were glazed and empty. Her hair was tangled and matted together, and she had the haunted look of someone who would never smile again.

'Why don't you kill me?' she repeated, as the van wended its way out of the residential area, with its low-rise apartments and small family homes surrounded by neatly mown lawns.

Gerald Gallego was only too pleased to oblige.

As summer gave way reluctantly to autumn and Sacramento breathed easy again in the fresher breeze blowing down from the mountains, Charlene observed her ever-growing bump with mixed feelings. On one hand she wanted a baby and she had some kind of crazy idea that bringing new life into the world would, in some way, wipe out the bad stuff that had gone before, as if she too could be reborn along with her baby. But things were hardly ideal at the moment. For one thing, she was back living with her parents. Gerry's mood swings and violence had got out of control and the couple had finally gone their separate ways, although she didn't believe she'd ever be able to leave him behind for good, not after all they'd been through. Not only this but she was becoming increasingly hooked on cocaine and didn't need to be told what a bad combination babies and drugs were.

When Charlene picked up the phone on the first day of November, she was surprised to hear Gerry's voice on the other end.

'I just wondered if you wanted to come out with me for the evening,' he asked her, tentatively, once again the polite, respectful guy he'd been when they first started dating. 'You know, just hang out. How we used to.'

Charlene hesitated. He'd acted so crazy the last few weeks they were together and she was almost sure he was seeing another woman. But as usual, she allowed herself to be swayed by him. He was still her husband after all, and the father of her baby. Why not spend some time together for old times' sake?

This was to prove one of the worst mistakes of Charlene's life.

At first everything was fine. They'd driven round to a few bars, catching up on all that had been happening in each other's lives. Well, edited highlights at least. Charlene wasn't stupid enough to tell her hot-headed ex exactly what she'd been up to; and Gerry, well, he'd long been of the opinion that whatever he did was his business and no one else's.

But as the evening wore on, Charlene noticed the familiar

telltale signs that meant her estranged husband was getting restless. His hands moved constantly as though rehearsing for something and his eyes, which had been the first thing to draw her to him, darted about edgily. As she drove into the car park of another shopping mall, where a brightly lit restaurant/bar showed signs of a party in progress, Charlene was overwhelmed with that same feeling of sick dread mixed with a kind of almost detached fascination. It was as though she was witness to an inevitable train crash. She could see the obstruction on the track, see the high speed engine hurtling ahead oblivious, but there wasn't nothing she could do about it. And even if there had been, she didn't know if she really wanted to.

The gaily decorated restaurant was the venue for a college dance being held by one of the fraternity houses at California State University of Sacramento. Waiting in a shadowy part of the car park with the headlights turned off, Charlene and Gerald could get a clear view of the students spilling out of the hot steamy party into the sudden chill of the early November night.

To Charlene, still just 23, the breathless girls in their long formal ball gowns, with their gleaming hair and their rosy futures that they wore pinned to them as visibly as their brightly coloured corsages, were a painful reminder of the world she'd left behind, the lost life that could have been hers.

Gradually the crowd of departing students thinned out until there was just the odd straggling pair, laughing at the unaccustomed gloom, men's jackets slung chivalrously over women's bare shoulders.

'Those two!'

Gerald's voice was barely audible. He was concentrating on a couple approaching a nearby Honda, his body like a cat about to pounce. And then he was out of the car, gun held close to his chest. Now the couple were in the back seat of the car, staring straight ahead, shock freezing their mouths into perfect round 'o's.

Crash!

The boy dropped his bunch of car keys out of the open window. Cursing, Charlene got out of the driver's seat and went round the other side of the car to find them, leaving Gerry in the front seat, his gun trained on the two reluctant passengers. Which is when Andy Beal, seeing his friends Craig and Mary Beth in the back of an unfamiliar car, went to investigate.

'Get the hell away from my car!' Charlene screeched, flying back round the car and landing a stinging slap on the side of the young man's face.

And then they were off, pulling out of the car park, the bemused stranger growing ever smaller in the rear view mirror, his hand still clutched to his face.

'That was really stupid,' Charlene hissed, her heart pounding painfully in her skinny chest.

'Shut up!'

Gerald never could take being called stupid.

As the car edged its way off the highway and into the hills out of town, where the only lights come from the odd farmhouse or the stars themselves, Gerry called to Charlene to stop.

'Do you want him?' he hissed, gesturing to Craig. She shook her head.

Then Craig Miller, acting on instructions from Gerald, and still clinging to the all-American rulebook that says if you do what you're told, you get rewarded, got out of the car and started walking uncertainly along the dark, silent road. Gerry got out after him. A shot was fired, and then two more.

Charlene tried not to look at the large shape lying motionless by the side of the road or to consider the girl in the back of the car, stiff and mute with fear – and with the growing realisation of what was about to happen to her.

'Let's go,' Gerry was back in the car. 'Back to my place!'

Inside the shabby apartment where Gerald had been living while separated from Charlene, he shoved the shaking student in her rustling formal gown ahead of him into the bedroom. Charlene, pumped full of resentment for all this girl had and all she herself had lost, followed behind.

The Mary Beth who saw the sun rise the next morning in the company of Mr and Mrs Gallego was almost unrecognisable from the assured, confident student who'd left the dance just hours before.

'We're going for another drive,' Gerald told her, gruffly, forcing her into the back seat behind he and Charlene. When the big Oldsmobile pulled back into the driveway a couple of hours later, there were only two people inside.

But that night, 2 November 1980, was when Gerald and Charlene's luck finally ran out. Andy Beal, standing alone and confused in a mall car park, his cheek still stinging from a slap he hadn't seen coming, had memorised the number plate. It didn't take long for the car to be traced back.

'I wasn't driving the car last night,' Charlene told the police officer who came to interview her. 'I was with my boyfriend in his car. His name is Stephen Feil.'

The police ran a check on Feil. A photocopy of his driving licence photograph was shown to Andy Beal, who immediately identified him as the man he'd seen with his friends the night before. When a call came in to say that Craig Miller's body had been found Stephen Feil went from being a suspect in an abduction to becoming the suspect in a murder case.

Gerald Gallego's apartment was searched, and he and Charlene decided to flee.

'It's all a mistake,' Charlene told her worried parents. 'They've got the wrong people.'

But the Williams weren't convinced. By now they were slowly realising what their son-in-law was accused of doing, and they were desperately concerned about their daughter's safety. Of course it wouldn't have occurred to them that she could be in any way implicated – not their little blonde princess.

They told police that Feil was an alias.

'The real name of the man you're looking for,' confided Chuck Williams, 'is Gerald Armand Gallego.'

This was the clue police had been looking for. Now, more than two years after the Gallegos first started kidnapping and murdering, things started to fall into place. A gun used by Gerald to shoot holes in the ceiling of a bar he'd once worked at was identified as the weapon that had killed Craig and Mary Beth.

Gerald and Charlene were on the run, but they wouldn't get far. On 17 November 1980, they approached the Western Union post office in Omaha, Nebraska, where Charlene had asked her parents to wire her some money. Gerry waited outside while she walked into the building alone to pick up the funds.

The police were waiting.

The Gallegos were charged with the murder of Craig Miller and Mary Beth Sower. For eighteen long months as police painstakingly collected evidence, they battled a wall of silence and denials from the couple.

'Your marriage to Gerry wasn't even legal,' they told Charlene, after discovering that he'd never bothered to divorce at least one of his previous wives. 'You can stand up against him in court.'

But she refused to listen.

Charlene had her baby – a boy – while in custody awaiting trial. It wasn't at all how she'd envisaged the birth of her first child. Her body ached for her son long after he was taken, screaming, from her to live with her parents.

She longed for Gerry but at the same time a part of her hated and blamed him. He was supposed to be her man, to look after her. Wouldn't someone who really loved her stand up and take the blame for everything? Surely he would do anything to see her released, unable to bear to think of her rotting away in a prison cell?

Irene Silverman was murdered by Kenny Kimes (*inset*) for her huge wealth. Kenny and his mother Sante were eventually found guilty of an astonishing 118 crimes between them. 

A man of pure evil. Marc Dutroux kidnapped, raped and killed young girls in a hidden dungeon he built in his basement. He was eventually found guilty of murder and sentenced to life imprisonment. © *PA Photos*

Michelle Martin, Dutroux's ex-wife, allowed two of Marc's victims to starve to death, for which she received thirty years in prison. © *PA Photos*

The underground dungeon where Dutroux kept his victims. Only two girls survived the ordeal – Laetitia Delhez and Sabine Dardenne (*inset*), who went on to publish a book about her 80 days of captivity at the hands of the notorious paedophile.

© *REX Features*

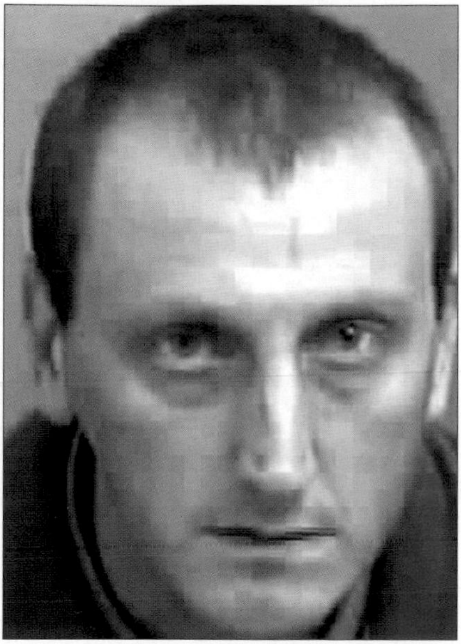

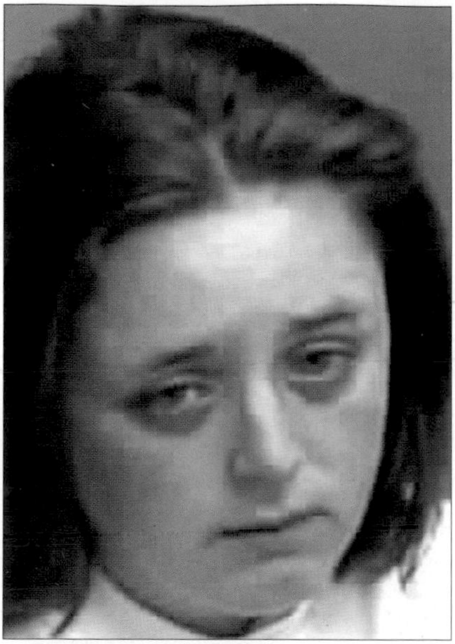

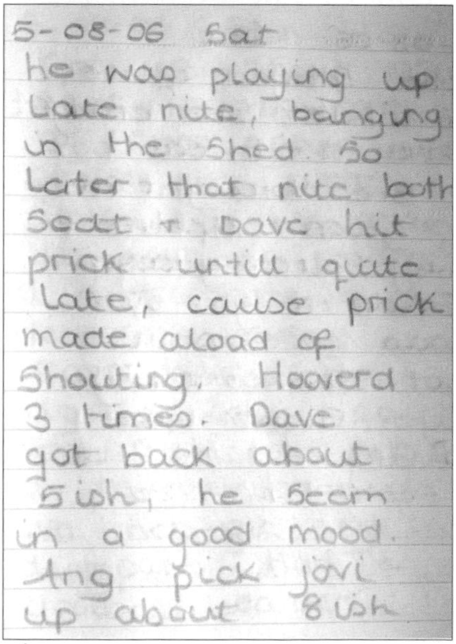

5-08-06 Sat
he was playing up
Late nite, banging
in the Shed so
Later that nite both
Scott + Dave hit
prick untill quate
Late, cause prick
made aload of
Shouting. Hooverd
3 times. Dave
got back about
5ish, he seem
in a good mood.
Ang pick jovi
up about 8ish

David Lehane (*top left*) and Amanda Baggus (*top right*) kidnapped their friend Kevin Davies and kept him prisoner in their garden shed for nearly four months (*bottom left*). During that time they physically and verbally abused him, as Amanda's secret diary recounted (*bottom right*); Kevin was eventually found dead by paramedics. *© REX Features*

The infamous Fred and Rose West, who were charged with twenty-two counts of murder between them. © *REX Features*

25 Cromwell Street where many of the victims were killed and later buried.

*© REX Features*

Some of the victims, including the West's own daughter, Heather, were buried in the garden.

*© REX Features*

At the beginning of March 1982, Charlene had a change of heart.

'Craig and Mary Beth weren't the first,' she told stunned detectives.

Charlene Gallego agreed to stand up in a court of law and tell the whole truth about what had happened, but she wanted something in return. The girl who'd so impressed her teachers at school with her intellect knew that her only hope of being able to walk out of prison alive and still with some good years ahead of her was to negotiate a plea bargain. The police wanted Gerald; she wanted a second chance at life. In the end, she was offered a sentence of sixteen years in return for telling everything she knew about Gerald Gallego.

And she knew plenty.

On 23 June 1983, Gerald Gallego was sentenced to death by a Californian court for the murders of Craig Miller and Mary Beth Sowers. A second trial in Nevada in May 1984 found him guilty of murdering Stacy Redican and Karen Twiggs. Again, he was sentenced to death.

He continued to protest his innocence despite all the evidence against him. The deaths had been in self defence, he claimed. He'd only meant to rob them.

Despite the two death sentences, Gerald Gallego's end, when it came, was from natural causes. On 17 July 2002, a hospital prison in Nevada announced that he'd passed away from rectal cancer.

Charlene Williams, the woman who'd called herself his wife,

who'd accompanied him on all his ill-fated kidnapping expeditions and eventually turned against him so crushingly at the end, walked away from prison a free woman in July 1997. She was not yet 40 years old.

Was she another victim or a willing accomplice who shared in Gerald Gallego's sick fantasies and enthusiastically helped him carry them out? Did she detach herself from what her 'husband' was doing, or participate enthusiastically, piling yet more agonies on the victims she'd helped lure into his path?

Somewhere in America, no one knows exactly where, there's a middle-aged woman, barely over five feet tall, whose child-like frame makes her appear vulnerable and in need of protection. She may still be looking for a man powerful enough to take care of her, a man she can look up to. She has a pretty, intelligent face but the wariness in her eyes speaks of a shadowy, difficult past.

Only she knows all the answers, but she's unlikely to tell you.

## CHAPTER 7

# SMOTHER LOVE

## SANTE AND KENNY KIMES

Despite the obvious age gap, the couple in front of the TV cameras were clearly besotted by one another. Constantly holding hands and stroking one another as they took turns to talk to the presenter of the *60 Minutes* programme, they seemed to take great comfort just from being close to each other.

He was a young guy, probably in his mid-twenties and handsome in a clean-cut, preppy kind of way. In his designer suit, he looked like the kind of guy you'd expect to be selling you expensive houses or trying to sweet-talk you into a luxury car you couldn't really afford. She was well into middle age, a fact she hadn't been able to disguise with her unsparing use of heavy make-up, accentuated by her sensible-looking, business-style clothes. Her unnaturally black hair offset the chalky white of her thickly powdered skin.

They were hardly the best-matched couple but because of the obvious bond between them you could forgive these two lovebirds the incongruities in their age and wish them well, if it wasn't for one thing: Sante and Kenny Kimes were mother and son – and they were about to stand trial for murder.

The body was bulky, and with the head and feet wrapped in plastic bin liners, the two men found it difficult to get a proper grip.

'Come on, on the count of three!'

With a concerted effort, they heaved their awkward burden into the open dumpster. In the gloom of a Los Angeles evening, the alleyway they were in seemed eerily silent, the rubbish bins and empty boxes just menacing shapes in the shadows.

'Right, let's get out of here.'

The relief, as Kenny Kimes slid in behind the wheel of his car and high-tailed it away from that alleyway, was almost tangible. It was as though he could feel himself growing lighter with every metre he put between himself and that thing in the dumpster. And then along with the relief came another feeling – exhilaration.

He'd done it, he'd done it for her!

For almost the first time in his short life, he felt he'd really proved himself to the woman he loved above any other. With his nerves almost buzzing with energy and euphoria, Kenny wanted to do something to mark the occasion, a grand gesture to show how much she meant to him and how much he was willing to do for her.

Passing a florist, he pulled into the side of the road.

'Give me the biggest bunch of flowers you've got,' he told the pretty girl behind the counter. 'A hundred dollars' worth!'

She was worth it, he reflected, as he winked at the flower girl and strode back out to his car, his arms full of exotic blooms.

His mother was worth it.

Growing up as the son of the flamboyant Sante Kimes hadn't exactly been a picnic for Kenny. Forget the enormous mansions where maids outnumbered family members; the swimming pools and the fancy holidays, the nice clothes and the chauffeur-driven cars. Yes, he had wanted for nothing materially, but Kenny had been deprived in other areas. Although his mother Sante and Kenny's millionaire father Ken adored him, they were always off here and there – on someone's yacht, at a weekend party. And with his half-brother Kent thirteen years older and mostly living away from home, he was left largely to his own devices.

It wasn't as if he had a gang of mates to fall back on either. Sante, who always told Kenny he was different and special, didn't allow him to attend school where he might have mixed with any old riff-raff. Instead she had him tutored at home and he was only allowed to play with a few children that she'd personally vetted.

'What do you need lots of friends for when you have me?' she'd ask, her heavily made-up eyes wide with sincerity. 'You're my whole world.'

That might have been true, but it wasn't a very stable world.

Glamorous, extrovert Sante, who prided herself on being a Liz Taylor lookalike and even pretended to be the famous actress on occasion, had come from a desperately poor background where she'd had to get by on her wits. The result was that even as a wealthy adult she was always running one scam or another, never satisfied with what she had. Her third husband, Ken Kimes, was loaded enough for her never to have to worry about money, but being a Californian housewife was never part of Sante's plan. Instead the couple continued to amass more money through various cons and fraudulent deals, living it up as they went.

Sante was a woman of frustrating contradictions – charming, funny and warm on one hand, but self-absorbed and cruel on the other. Having lacked for so much as a child, she now made up for it by fashioning her life into the Sante Kimes show, with everyone else as supporting actors, just grateful to be able to warm themselves within the outer rings of her radiance.

As much as Sante could love anyone, she loved her children, particularly her younger son Kenny. In her typical vain, self-centred way, Sante never really believed Kenny existed in an independent state – only as an offshoot of herself, a wonderful artwork she personally had created.

Right from the word go, she watched over what he wore, who he mixed with. Whenever she could, she had him with her: talking to him, moulding his views to her own. And Kenny, knowing nothing else and in thrall, as so many people were, to the force of nature that was Sante, was by and large happy to be moulded.

By the time Kenny was a teenager, his beloved mother was in jail. She was found guilty of two separate crimes – one of stealing a mink coat, another of slavery. Incredible though it sounded in 1980s California, Sante had recruited impoverished girls off the streets in Mexico and brought them to the US with promises of a steady income, only to keep them imprisoned in her homes, forcing them to work for nothing and beating them at whim. One even claimed to have been branded with a hot iron. She served five years in prison.

But if that period of enforced separation gave Kenny a taste of independent life away from his controlling mother's clutches, he was back under her spell the moment she was released in 1989.

The thing was, Sante Kimes just had something about her. Though capable of great cruelty, she was also warm, charismatic and generous to those she loved. Being with her was never dull. She was always looking out for the next adventure, the next thrill, and her impressionable young son was swept right along with her.

By the time Kenny started at the University of California in Santa Barbara in August 1993, his close relationship with his mother was already raising eyebrows. 'It's not natural for a young guy like that to spend so much time with his mother,' friends would whisper. Tongues wagged faster still when Sante insisted on moving with Kenny when he started college, sharing a house with him off-campus, where she played hostess to student parties, mingling with his friends as though she were his girlfriend rather than his mother. Rumour had it that when the family went on holiday, it was Kenny and Sante who shared a double room while Ken slept alone.

Sante and Ken loved each other but it was a destructive kind of love. They brought out the worst in each other, and Ken always knew that the relationship between his wife and their son was unnaturally close. Indeed, there was a constant power struggle when he was alive between him and Sante over who could have most influence over Kenny.

When Ken died of a heart attack in 1994 Sante, well aware that her husband hadn't changed his first Will made before he met her, didn't tell anyone. Instead, she continued to forge his name on documents and told anyone who asked that he was away doing business abroad. Now that it was just Kenny and Sante their relationship, always close, became claustrophobic. If he was her world, she was also his. Handsome, charming young Kenny would do anything for his mother.

In 1996, the pair flew out to the Bahamas to meet with Syed Bilal Ahmed – a banker whom Sante was sure would help her secure a loan. It was an offer Ahmed could, and did, refuse. Shortly afterwards, he disappeared. Kenny would later admit in court that he'd drugged Ahmed and then he and Sante had held him down in the bathtub until he'd drowned. His weighted-down body had then been tossed into the ocean. No body, no crime…

David Kazdin was an old friend of Ken Kimes who agreed to help Sante out by putting his name on the deeds of one of her properties. However, when Sante secretly took out a massive mortgage on the property, which Kazdin was then expected to repay, he threatened to go to the authorities.

Sante's response was as unequivocal as it was callous: 'We're gonna have to kill him.'

On 13 March 1998, Kenny and a drifter he'd recruited to help went to Kazdin's luxurious Los Angeles home.

'David, I need to talk to you about some things,' Kenny told the older man. But as Kazdin turned to get him a coffee, Kenny shot him in the back of the head. Later, he and his accomplice dumped Kazdin's body in a dumpster near Los Angeles airport. He then stopped to buy his mommy dearest a bunch of flowers.

'I felt I had completed a great duty,' he would later explain to a packed courtroom.

With the heat on, Kenny and Sante fled across America, writing dodgy cheques as they went. They had no plan of what to do next but Sante, ever the optimist, was sure something would come up. And it did. In Florida, they were told about an elderly Manhattan socialite who lived alone and rented out suites in her sumptuous New York mansion.

Irene Silverman may have been 83 years old, but she wasn't going to let a little thing like age get in the way of having a good time. The high-living widow, who owed her fortune to her property mogul husband, had converted her imposing grey limestone mansion at 20 East 65th Street, New York City, into a kind of luxury B&B for the rich and famous, where suites cost up to $6,000 per month. Even so, she didn't let just anyone stay, preferring those who came with a recommendation, or anyone who was fun to have around and happy to join her for dinner at one of her favourite restaurants or to accompany her to a party.

When a young man came to see her about renting an apartment in June 1998, Irene was suspicious. But the man, calling himself Manny Guerin, mentioned the name of one of her oldest friends by way of recommendation. It also didn't hurt that he offered her $6,000 in cash to stay in one of her suites.

'I'm expecting my PA any day. I hope that's OK?' he asked her, flashing her what was intended to be a winning smile.

But Irene was too long in the tooth to be taken in that easily. There was just something about the young man with the aquiline nose and the easy West Coast charm that put her on edge. And things didn't improve when his PA arrived. The dumpy, middle-aged woman with the impossibly black hair and loud rasping voice soon put the backs up all Irene's loyal staff and so the old lady decided to keep a watchful eye on the suspicious pair and keep a written journal of her observations.

The weekend of 4 July is one of the biggest celebrations in the US calendar. Irene had given all her staff the weekend off to spend with their families and the Silverman mansion was uncharacteristically quiet. During the night of 4 July, while the rest of the city celebrated 223 years of independence, Irene's latest guests kept to their room, where they could be heard talking and arguing. But at some point during that night, the door to their suite opened and someone let themselves out softly. Soon after, 83-year-old Irene Silverman was bundled into her own bedroom, where a struggle ensued. She was shot in the head with a stun gun and then young Mr Guerin strangled her with his bare hands.

Except, of course, that his name wasn't Manny Guerin: it was Kenny Kimes. And his loud, brash PA was none other than his mother Sante.

The plan had been simple – and breathtakingly arrogant. They'd murder Irene, then pretend that the old lady had gone off on a long vacation and had sold her house to her 'dear friend' Sante. She would even forge a Bill of Sale to back up the story. Every stage of the planning was jotted down in one of the notebooks Sante took everywhere with her.

Once Irene was dead, the couple wrapped her tiny, frail body in a shower curtain specially bought for the task and crammed it into a large case, which they then hauled downstairs and out onto the street. Luckily for them, New York City was sleeping off its collective hangover by this time and hardly anyone was around to witness the mismatched couple heaving their heavy suitcase into the boot of their Lincoln car.

'No body, no crime,' Sante always said, and the two went to great lengths to make sure Irene Silverman would never be found, driving all the way to New Jersey to dispose of the body in a rubbish container in Hoboken.

But back in New York City, their luck was about to run out. A few days before the murder, they'd called a contact of theirs in Las Vegas. Stan Patterson had done 'odds and ends' for them before, not all of them strictly legal, so they were sure they could trust him.

'We're thinking of opening up a luxury B&B in New York City,' Sante told him. 'How'd you like to run it for us?'

Nothing Sante Kimes did surprised Patterson, but equally he wasn't too surprised to find the police at his door soon after that conversation, asking about the murder of a guy named David Kazdin, a stolen car and a trail of other things that all seemed to point in one direction: Sante and Kenny Kimes.

When Scott turned up to meet Sante and Kenny at the New York Hilton, on 5 July 1998, he was not alone.

'You can't do this, we're completely innocent – get your hands off me!' Sante played the outraged citizen to perfection. Kenny, meanwhile, was wetting himself. Literally.

A search of the couple's car soon turned up some interesting finds for the arresting officers. There were two guns, syringes, handcuffs and pepper spray. In addition, there was a wealth of evidence pertaining to a certain Irene Silverman – passport, keys, social security card and, most damning of all, a deed to her house with what was later proved to be a forged signature, reporting transfer of the ownership of the property to a corporation set up by Sante herself. There were also notebooks in Sante's handwriting, in which she jotted down questions about the old lady's habits and practised copying her signature.

The haul was to take on an extra significance when it was discovered that Irene Silverman had gone missing that same day.

'Those things aren't ours,' Sante insisted. 'They were planted there. This is a complete miscarriage of justice!'

It was to become a familiar refrain while she and Kenny sat in custody in New York City waiting for trial. The body of Irene Silverman had never been found and Sante continued to proclaim their innocence, claiming all the evidence against she and her son had been manufactured.

'It's the worst mistake in US justice history,' she repeated to anyone who would listen.

Never exactly shrinking violets the Kimes courted publicity for their cause, giving interviews to TV presenters and magazine feature writers alike in the hope of drumming up public support. 'There is no crime, there is no body, there is no evidence,' Sante would repeat, her voice shrill with self-righteous anger. 'This is a witch hunt!'

People may not have bought the 'poor maligned me' act, in fact the duo were quickly dubbed 'Mommy and Clyde' after the legendary gangster couple of the 1930s. But the one thing no one doubted was Sante's extravagant concern for her boy, her Kenny.

'He's going through hell on earth, hell on earth,' she lamented to CNN's Larry King. 'The only reason I'm alive is that I must prove his innocence… He is as wonderful a son as you could ever pray for.'

Kenny was equally effusive. 'My mom is a wonderful, caring mother,' he told Larry King during the same show. 'Her world is me, and she is my world.'

Many viewers felt a strange chill at his words. Though both mother and son vehemently denied the persistent rumours of an incestuous relationship, somehow Kenny's proclamation of filial love didn't seem natural. How many good-looking 24-

year-old men would go on national TV and admit that their mothers were their whole lives?

In prison, Sante bombarded her son with letters, giving him advice on how to cope with the pressure. These letters invariably started with an endearment such as 'Kenny, my soul mate son' or 'My honey bunny'. A veteran of court appearances, she warned him against looking cold. 'The key is to show good emotions,' she wrote. 'Just like a sweet little beaten puppy.'

Like his mother, Kenny denied any wrongdoing. They were scapegoats, he echoed. They were simply in the wrong place at the wrong time.

But the jury didn't believe them. In May 2000, Sante and Kenny Kimes were found guilty of an incredible 118 crimes between them, the most serious of which was the murder of Irene Silverman. Just reading out the verdicts took twenty minutes. Sante was sentenced to 120 years in prison, her darling Kenny to 125.

The judge called Sante 'the most degenerate defendant who has ever appeared in this court room,' while Kenny was described as a 'vacuous dupe'.

As she left the court, Sante was still screaming her innocence, declaring the whole process a catastrophic miscarriage of justice.

So what went through the minds of the two as they were driven to their respective prisons, knowing they were going to spend the rest of their lives behind bars and, worst of all, be separated from one another? Did self-obsessed self-serving Sante ever blame herself for what she'd done to her son? Did she think of him, just 25, with his whole life ahead of him, and cry for the future she'd robbed him of, for the girls he'd never marry, the children he'd never father?

The answer is probably no. Sante was living the Sante Kimes Show, don't forget. She was the star and whatever lines she spouted at the time were the ones she believed. Sante probably did think she was innocent and that the police had framed her and Kenny; that she was a fantastic mother whose son was happy to be close to her. She never understood that their relationship overstepped any boundaries simply because she didn't believe the boundaries existed in the first place. In Sante's eyes, it was herself and Kenny against the world. Not in a million years would she accept that she was responsible for setting the world against Kenny.

And what of Kenny, alone in his prison cell, slowly facing up to the enormity of what he'd done and to the fact that this was to be his life from now on? Did he ever ask himself how differently his life might have turned out if he'd had a regular mother who brought him up to know that the world had rules, and then set him free to negotiate his own way around them? Did he ever wonder what kind of parent shows their love by suffocating their child, or by acting like a girlfriend rather than a mother?

Whatever went through his head in his long dark night of the soul, Kenny Kimes remained fiercely devoted to his high spirited, gregarious mama. In excerpts from his diary, published in an accompanying magazine interview, he talked of 'dreamy images of me and Mom, walking down the beach together hand in hand, walking into the sunset.'

The thing that worried him most was the threat of extradition to California to face charges over David Kazdin's murder. As long as they stayed in New York, they'd serve out their life sentences in prison, but if they were found guilty of murder by a court in California, they could find themselves facing the death penalty. The thought of that happening to himself or his beloved Sante was too much for Kenny to bear.

On 10 October 2000, Kenny was in the process of being interviewed by a female news reporter when he whipped out a pen he'd borrowed from a guard and pressed it into the woman's neck, effectively holding her hostage. He didn't want to die and his mother was too old to be executed, he told the shocked guards and onlookers: he wanted a guarantee that they wouldn't be extradited – and a ride to Canada.

In the end he got neither. After a tense four hours a shaking, desperate Kenny Kimes was overpowered by guards, his hostage released unharmed. He was rewarded for his stunt with eight years in solitary confinement, an eternity for a man whose contemporaries were still partying every Saturday night or taking their first tentative steps towards marriage and babies.

Kenny hadn't really had a chance to get used to life in solitary before he was on the move again. All his efforts had been for nothing; he and Sante were going to California to face murder charges.

It was back in California, where they'd once lived fast and free on a diet of champagne and thrillseeking that the bonds between mother and son finally began to unravel. Kenny desperately didn't want to die. He knew he was unlikely ever to be free, but faced with the prospect of never going out to dinner with a beautiful girl or running into the sea with the sun on his face, he still chose life. But to escape the death penalty, he needed a bargaining chip, and the only one he had was his mother.

In November 2002, Kenny Kimes pleaded guilty to first degree murder and agreed to give evidence against his mother in return for a guarantee that neither of them would face execution. By this stage he'd had enough time alone to realise some uncomfortable truths about his relationship with the woman who'd shaped his life, who'd been his life. What Kenny was starting to understand was that it is possible to love someone and to destroy them at the same time. Sante had adored him – she'd lavished him with affection, with money, with the kind of lifestyle that makes a young, shallow boy feel like he's worth something – but in so doing, she'd taken from him everything that was his own and made him who he was. She'd shown him a passion as intense as it was inappropriate, and in return she'd demanded everything. Sante's love was as big as an ocean, as high as a mountain, but it came with a massive price tag: for the honour of being her son, companion and, some implied, her lover as well, Kenny had to buy wholesale into Sante's world, where money was worth less than people and laws only applied to others.

In a strange sense, it took being locked up behind bars in

solitary confinement for Kenny to truly be freed. Away from Sante's influence, finally he could sever the umbilical cord and start to breathe independently for the first time. He still loved his mother, but he'd stopped seeing the world through her eyes and he wanted to live. Surely she couldn't deny him that much?

In June 2004, a shackled and beaten-looking Kenny Kimes shuffled into a Californian courtroom to give evidence against his mother. Though still only 29, he had the gaunt, haunted appearance of a man twice his age and the tears, never far from his green eyes, gave them a rheumy look normally seen only in the elderly.

His mother, who insisted on coming to court in a wheelchair despite not having a definable medical complaint, still complained her love loudly for the broken man in the regulation orange prison jumpsuit. He'd been brainwashed, she told anyone who would listen. They'd tortured him until he confessed.

By this stage Sante Kimes too had changed almost beyond recognition. Her trademark black hair, which people had used to say put them in mind of Elizabeth Taylor, was now short and grey, her face plump, with round cheeks that were quick to flush red. She peered out around the courtroom through large, white-lensed glasses, her gaze always coming back to rest on the lone figure in the orange jumpsuit, as if willing him to look at her. She could have been anyone's benign, beloved grandmother. Instead, after she'd been found guilty, the judge declared her 'one of the most evil individuals' she'd ever come across. Kenny, she added, had been another one of her victims.

When Sante, alongside her son, was sentenced to life without possibility of parole, her shrieks of outrage seemed to still echo around the courtroom long after she'd been led away.

Sante and Kenny Kimes may have been mother and son, but they behaved like a romantic couple, with Sante calling the shots and Kenny following devotedly and powerlessly behind. By keeping him apart from his peers, controlling his every move and showering him with extravagant gifts and even more abundant displays of affection, Sante sought to create in her son an idealised companion and soul mate, perhaps even a lover. The tragedy is that in so doing, she also created a monster – in that at least, the two were well matched.

## CHAPTER 8

# DUNGEONS OF THE MIND

## MARC DUTROUX AND MICHELLE MARTIN

Michelle Martin picked her way fearfully down the dark stairs. In the damp, oppressive silence the only sounds she could hear were the occasional movements of the two restless Alsatian dogs upstairs, plus the pounding of her own heart.

The bags containing water bottles and various packets of food swung awkwardly from her hand as she descended further into the fuggy gloom, her apprehension increasing with each step. And here was the basement, close and airless, the odd jar or bottle or lumpy sack giving it an abandoned, uncared for feel. The shape of an upside down letter 'L', the basement walls were formed on all except one side by crumbling brick. The other wall was covered in white plastic panels, fronted with shelves. That was the wall that disguised the door to the dungeon.

Now other sounds came wafting through the suffocating,

dank air, the sounds of children whispering. Michelle was really nervous, her thin fingers fidgeting anxiously with the handle of the bags. So they were there, behind the door – awake, listening, conspiring. What would they say to her? What would they do?

She imagined them flying at her, screaming, accusing… How would she look them in the eyes? How could she turn her back on them and walk back through the hole, knowing what she knew? Knowing who they were, seeing the terror in their faces? The raw, savage animal fear.

They'd be like wild things, she told herself fearfully. They'd attack her. She couldn't take the chance.

Stomach churning, she pulled aside the plastic panelling and heaved the 200-kilo cement door open. It was not enough to see anything, certainly not enough for them to get to her. Quickly she shoved the water bottles and the bags of food into the hole that led to the cellar. It'd be all right, she told herself, relief and revulsion coursing through her as she pulled the door shut again. Marc was bound to have left them with enough provisions to survive. And she couldn't be expected to go in there again; it was too dangerous. What if they went for her? What if they escaped? Marc would kill her if they weren't there when he got back. Hurriedly, she rearranged the panelling to cover up any sign of a door and shoved two sacks of coal against it.

It wasn't her fault, she told herself. It was Marc's fault, all of it. Yes, she was supposed to be feeding them but it wasn't she who had brought them here. Besides, there wasn't anything she could do for them. She had her own children to protect.

And so Michelle Martin decided not to go there again. She'd come back to feed the dogs, but not go back down into the basement where wild beasts lurked in cellar holes, waiting to torment her. She'd wipe from her memory the sound of children whispering through cement walls, the thought, quickly quashed, of small bodies slowly starving away to nothing. They weren't human, these presences in the cellar – not like her own children. Best to forget all about them.

And so two 8-year-old girls slowly starved to death in a filthy, damp underground cellar, their names crayoned on the wall in their childish writing, the only testament to their last bleak days. Because the man who'd kidnapped them and kept them as sex slaves had gone away and the woman he'd asked to feed them convinced herself that they weren't human to save her own skin.

When adult relationships become sufficiently twisted, other people, even small children, count for nothing – servants of their whims, or collateral damage in a private power struggle.

Michelle Martin was a good skater. Whenever she could, the young woman would head for the local skating rink, near her home just outside Brussels, losing herself for a while in the loud music, the excitement of streaking across the ice, feeling her skates slice through the surface like the blade of a knife. It was a way of escaping her overprotective mother for a while, and it was also a great way of meeting men.

One day in 1983, her attention was caught by a man working his way across the ice. He was older than her, with black hair and swarthy features, but he moved with such effortless grace and skill that she was quite mesmerised. The next time she went, she noticed him again, and after a while she began to look out for him, secretly hoping to spot his black hair so clearly offset against the white background.

Trainee teacher Michelle was a pretty blonde of just 20, with delicate features and a slim, almost fragile frame, and she soon attracted the attention of the mystery skater. The two began chatting.

Marc Dutroux was unlike anyone Michelle had ever met. To her, he seemed so charismatic and charming, and so interested in her. A reserved, slightly nervous character, she'd never had anyone pay attention to her the way Marc did, as if he was truly listening to what she said.

Soon the couple began meeting outside of the skating rink. Michelle told him how fed up she was at home and how she'd always felt her mother blamed her for her father's death in a car accident while he was driving her to school. With Marc she felt desirable, young and reckless. He seemed so worldly, so sophisticated. She couldn't believe a man like him had singled her out.

Of course there was a catch. Marc Dutroux was already married, with two young sons. Not only that, he had at least one other lover as well. But by the time Michelle found out, she was already madly in love. More than in love, she was completely infatuated, unable to contemplate a future without him in her life.

'I don't care about the other women, as long as we can be together,' she told him.

When Marc's wife found them in bed together and walked out, Michelle was secretly glad. Now she could move in with him and be the number one woman in his life. She could learn to live with his womanising, she told herself, as long as he came home to her at night.

But life with Marc Dutroux was to prove far from the fairytale she'd been promising herself. For one thing, he was very volatile. One minute he could be charming, attentive and loving, the next he'd be in a violent rage about something, pushing her roughly around the house they shared in Charleroi, Southern Belgium. Sex too was often brutal, his face contorted into an expression much more to do with power than love.

Then there was his 'work'. Though an electrician by trade, he seemed to do few jobs of that kind. Instead the phone rang all day with men who talked in low voices and cryptic phrases. Gradually she gathered that he was involved with car theft and drug dealing. And yet she stayed with him, by this time hooked on the adrenaline rush of being with him, terrified at the idea of being alone.

Being with him was like an addiction. No matter how badly he treated her, or what dark secrets she learned about him, Michelle always came back for more. She knew he'd had a miserable childhood, living with a man who wasn't his real father and a mother he insisted didn't like him. He'd run away, even worked as a rent boy, learning all the ways in which sex can be turned into a commercial commodity, the prices people would pay for their own gratification or someone else's degradation.

Yes, she knew he was terminally unfaithful. Waiting up for him at night, she'd know exactly where he was – parking his camper van by the ice rink, hoping to pick up a woman there, who was willing to have sex with him on the mattress in the back.

'Why can't you just stay home with me?' she'd plead. 'Why aren't I enough?'

But Marc would only gaze at her with brown eyes that burned with disdain.

'I told you I needed my independence,' he'd hiss at her, making her feel parochial, narrow-minded and petty.

'I understand. I love you,' her words would come out in a rush, so desperate was she to win his good favour back, to have him smile at her again.

And so slowly, Michelle Martin, dedicated primary school teacher, started to lose her grip on what was right and what was wrong, what was acceptable and what should have caused immediate outrage. Even so, when Marc first mentioned kidnapping, she was shocked.

'If I just take a girl instead of wasting time hanging round the ice rink hoping to pick one up, it'll give me more time to spend with you,' he explained, as if it were the most logical thing in the world.

'You're joking, right?' she asked.

But Dutroux didn't joke about things like that. Instead he started to snatch girls off the street to drug and rape in the back of his van. Michelle Martin's moral compass slipped still further: first when she discovered the attacks but stayed silent, and then when she was dragged along to be an accomplice, driving the van to make the girls less suspicious when they pulled up.

It was as if all free will had been surrendered: no longer could she remember a time when life was black and white, a time when there were things you did and things that you'd never in a million years consider doing. She couldn't remember a time when she looked at her reflection and knew who she was. It was surprising how quickly she ceased to be affected by the terror in a girl's eyes, or the way she might gaze at Michelle in horrified, mute appeal, trying to block out the terrible things being done to her body. It was surprising how quickly she became immune to suffering, even started to enjoy it.

Eventually, in 1986, the couple were arrested and charged with the savagely violent kidnap and rape of five girls, the youngest just 12, and one 50-year-old woman, who had had a razor blade inserted into her vagina. At their trial in 1989, Michelle received a five-year sentence, Marc thirteen years. He was allowed out in 1992 just three years later - a fact which enraged his own mother, Jeanine Lauwens.

'Please don't release this man,' she pleaded with prison authorities. 'I have known for a long time my eldest son's temperament. What I do not know, and what all those who know him fear, is what he has in mind for the future.'

But her pleas fell on deaf ears.

Dutroux and Martin had got married while incarcerated in jail in 1989 and were reunited on their release from prison. Michelle soon became pregnant and gave birth to a son, the first of three children they'd have together. But if she thought that becoming a father again would rein in her husband's sickening activities, she was much mistaken.

In addition to trading in stolen cars and drug dealing, Marc became involved in selling young girls into prostitution. He travelled widely around Europe and was gone for lengthy periods. The financial rewards were substantial. Marc owned seven different properties around Belgium, some rented out, others used as the settings for pornographic movies. He had a network of male acquaintances, to whom he spoke at length about his 'business'.

By now Michelle was so deeply entrenched in her husband's seedy private life that she'd stopped seeing it from any other perspective but his own. Forget the life she'd known before, this was normality, this twilight world of shady men and frightened-looking girls, of grainy barbarities played out on an amateur video. Never a strong character, she no longer had the power of will to question him. Even if she had, she now knew enough of his violence not to even attempt to do so. Instead, she surrendered herself to him: Marc was in charge and he could deal with the questions of conscience, the logistics, the calls in the night... She had her children to keep her busy. Besides, she liked the money, the big houses and the smart parties to which they were invited by her husband's underworld contacts.

And so Michelle Martin sat back and did nothing, morally bankrupting herself, even while her bank balance swelled. But even Michelle, to whom rape and brutality were now as commonplace as studying and skating had once been, was not prepared for Marc's announcement in 1994 that he wanted to kidnap more girls, this time keeping them prisoner in one of his houses, not his van, for weeks, not hours. There were other people involved, he intimated – people who'd pay well for girls kidnapped to order.

'I'm not going to prison again,' Michelle told him angrily.

But Dutroux didn't pay any attention. Instead he started on some 'modifications' to his house in Marcinelle, near Charleroi. He was building a hidden dungeon.

Poking about in the dank basement, Rene Michaux stopped for a minute. There it was again, the sound of a child talking.

The policeman remained motionless, alert, but his eyes darted around the room, taking in the crumbling brick walls, on all except one side. There was no window anywhere through which voices might carry from the street, no door to another room, just shelves filled with bottles and sacks of coal.

'Did you hear that?' he asked the locksmith accompanying him on the search of the house in Marcinelle.

The other man nodded. He'd clearly heard not one, but two girls' voices.

At that moment one of Michaux' colleagues came thudding down the stairs.

'Silence,' he called, and for a moment no one moved, each man straining to hear something, anything.

But no other sounds came.

Eventually the police officers gave up and moved away, relieved to get out of that airless, cheerless place. Later, when they checked the back garden and saw children's clothes hanging on a neighbours' washing line, Michaux reassured himself that the voices had just been kids playing outside.

Through a hidden door in the wall, the wall so different from the others, two 8-year-old girls sat in chains, waiting for the rescue that never came.

Their names were Julie Lejeune and Melissa Russo. Until 24 June 1995, they were ordinary schoolgirls, best friends who giggled and argued, who rode bikes and drew pictures with bright coloured crayons. And then one day, while playing on an overpass near Melissa's home in Grace-Hollogne, Liege, where they'd gone to wave to the lorry drivers passing underneath, they disappeared. Two little girls were gone in a heartbeat, their high-pitched laughter wafting gently on the summer breeze.

Their disappearance sparked a massive search, with their distraught families growing increasingly desperate as the days passed, but no clues were found. They had simply vanished.

When Marc Dutroux and his accomplice Bernard Weinstein brought the girls home to Marcinelle they were taken aback at how young they were. In their haste to kidnap two girls – according to Michelle Martin to order for others in their shady network – they hadn't properly sized up their age. Nevertheless, they were bundled into the hidden dungeon behind the cellar wall, a narrow cell, barely 9 by 3ft, with bare light bulbs and a rancid mattress, and a ventilation system of which Dutroux was immensely proud, completely undetectable from the outside.

The terrified children were then shackled to the wall and closed in, their sobs unheeded behind the heavy concrete barrier.

No one knows exactly what happened to Julie and Melissa over the long days, weeks and months that followed. Certainly they were sexually abused, forced to witness and endure things no 8-year-old should ever know existed, even in nightmares. Certainly they cried in the night for the families they'd left behind, dreaming of waking up safe in their own beds again, of playing in sun-dappled streets where children's screams were signs of over-excitement, not terror or rape. Was the abuse carried out by Marc Dutroux alone, or did others join in his sadistic pleasure? Who bought and distributed the videotapes he almost certainly made of his brutal, sordid attacks? Did Julie and Melissa stay in their underground hell the whole time, or were they loaned out to be playthings in a wider paedophile network? No one knows for sure. The walls can't talk, and the people who can are either discredited, or dead.

Though he had his two child prisoners in the cellar, Marc Dutroux was not satisfied. He hadn't intended to snatch such young girls; he needed to find other sex slaves – older, more womanly... After all, he wasn't a paedophile, or rather he wasn't *exclusively* a paedophile – he was just a man who got sexual kicks from power and complete domination.

Eefje Lambrecks, 19, and An Marchal, 17, were holidaying with a group of friends near Ostend on the Belgian coast when they decided to take a trip to the nearby town of Blankenberge to see a hypnotism show. But the show finished much later than expected and the tram they took home dropped them off a long way from their holiday bungalow in Westende.

'Don't hitchhike,' the tram driver warned them, worried about two young, attractive girls walking alone in the dark. 'Take a taxi!'

In the end, as always, it was all about timing. A moment or two earlier or later, and Eefje and An would have trudged off into the night and arrived breathlessly back at their bungalow, bursting with funny stories to share with their friends about what had happened in the show. If only they'd left before the end and caught an earlier tram, they'd have finished off their holiday and returned home to their families, ready to start the next adventure of their lives – An to return to school, Eefje to take up her place on a journalism degree course. Instead, they came across Marc Dutroux.

Marc was with another of his accomplices, Michel Lelièvre, when they kidnapped Eefje and An on 22 August 1995. Lelièvre was a pornographer and a junkie, willing to do anything for another fix. Together the two men overpowered the girls with chloroform and forced them into their van.

Drugged and helpless, they were transported back to

Dutroux' home in Marcinelle, where they were taken to a room above the same cellar dungeon in which the two traumatised 8-year-olds still huddled together, whispering in the long damp nights. Stripped naked, they were tied to the bed there in that room of nightmares. And again started the rapes, the videotaping and the systematic, soul-destroying abuse accompanied by the gradual realisation that no one was coming to save them, that this was their reality.

Under Marc's orders, Michel Lelièvre stood outside the room where the girls were held captive, talking loudly about a gang who wanted to kill them because their parents refused to pay a ransom. Then Dutroux himself came in to assuage their fears, promising to protect them, playing the role of saviour, wanting them to be grateful to him, to think well of him...

Marc Dutroux was an arrogant man, a bully, convinced of his own superiority. He didn't see that what he was doing as wrong, in fact he told himself that, in Eefje's case at least, it was a relationship, rather than an assault.

'Eefje was consenting,' he would tell a shocked courtroom, years later. 'But probably because she was trying to soften me up to get something. She was a nice girl.'

Despite his imagined closeness with his captive, Dutroux knew that the two teenagers would have to go. With the dungeon still occupied by Julie and Melissa, it was only a question of time before the other girls either escaped or were rescued. Eefje had already made one attempt to flee, opening a bathroom window and shouting for help. He couldn't risk them being spotted.

'You're going home,' he told the incredulous girls one day. 'I'm going to give you sleeping pills for the journey so that you can't describe where you've been.' Hardly daring to believe it, the two teenaged friends took the tablets he gave them – they were Rhohypnol, known as the date rape drug because it leaves the user in a waking trance, able to be manipulated, but not to move independently or remember what has happened. But instead of taking them home, Dutroux and Weinstein took the girls to one of his other houses outside Charleroi. There, the still breathing girls were dumped in shallow graves in the garden, which were then covered with concrete. One was still conscious.

'She was awake,' he later told Michelle, tears shining in his normally emotionless brown eyes. 'She knew she was going to die.'

But he buried the girls anyway. Later, Weinstein would also share the same fate, buried alive at the hand of Dutroux. He'd first been tortured by having a metal wire tightened around his testicles, probably over the whereabouts of a stash of money.

'I have good news and bad news,' Marc Dutroux told his wife afterwards. 'The good news is that I've bought you a mobile home. The bad news is that I had to suppress Bernard – he knew too much.'

By this stage nothing Michelle Martin's husband did shocked her any more. He inhabited a netherworld outside the rules of ordinary people, where nothing was unthinkable, and everything was for sale. And she lived right down there alongside him, enabling him in his atrocities, even joining in with him. A mother, a former teacher, she'd now become a woman who sat by and did nothing while children suffered and cried to go home.

To Michelle Martin, Marc Dutroux was a kind of toxic Svengali figure – a man who'd taken a weak, pliable young woman and bound her to him, moulding her into a sex criminal with a moral vacuum instead of a heart. It seemed to her that he could get away with anything, even murder. In this she was not far wrong, because since 1993, Marc Dutroux had owed his continued freedom to what was either a series of monumental bureaucratic mistakes or, as many people would come to believe, a systematic official cover-up.

Back in 1993, Claude Thirault, a police informant, told the authorities how he'd been offered £3,500 to kidnap a child – and the man who made the offer? Marc Dutroux. Thirault further told police how Dutroux was building underground cells in his houses to hold children before selling them on abroad. Police actually searched three of Dutroux' homes, where they found evidence of substantial alterations to the basement of one, but still nothing was done.

The following year, a man arrested in Holland on a charge of sexually abusing three children, poured his heart out to police, telling them of a paedophile ring based in Charleroi in Belgium. Again, no charges were made.

In 1995, Dutroux's mother Jeanine once again became sufficiently troubled by reports of her oldest son to write a letter to the police. Neighbours at one of his houses reported seeing two teenage girls outside in the back garden, she wrote. But these girls were only ever seen at night. He'd been having work done on his cellar, there were comings and goings all through the night… She was very much afraid he was keeping young girls captive.

Again police were slow to act, but that wasn't the only context in which Dutroux's name was mentioned to the authorities in 1995. He was also coming up in investigations into large-scale car theft and fraud. A police investigation, codenamed Operation Othello, was launched. It was while the police supposedly had Marc Dutroux under surveillance that he managed to abduct Eefje and An. They were still watching him when Eefje made her brave, but futile attempt to escape, and again when he took the girls to another of his houses to be buried.

And the police noticed nothing.

At the beginning of December 1995, Marc Dutroux was brought before a Belgian court of law, not for kidnapping or murder, but car theft. He was convicted of the charge and received a prison sentence. Before it began, he had an urgent message for his wife, Michelle.

'Make sure you feed the girls,' he told her. 'And the dogs.'

Just a week later, the police made that search of Dutroux's house in Marcinelle, hearing children's voices in the cellar but failing to link them to the newly finished wall at one end, or to wonder why a basement that should have been rectangular was now shaped like an 'L'. Neither did they think to question the unsavoury items they found there – vaginal cream, handcuffs and a speculum of the kind used in gynaecological examinations. Nor did they watch any of the videotapes stored there, which would later be found to contain footage of Dutroux constructing his dungeon and raping young girls. Instead they walked away, their footsteps fading into nothing. And Julie and Melissa were left alone.

Now Michelle Martin was faced with a nightmare. She'd promised to give food and water to the girls imprisoned in the cellar, but the thought of going near it revolted her. Only once did she manage to control her fears enough to go down the stairs to where the clammy air felt moist with decay and desolation. With shaking hands, she manoeuvred open the door to the hole, normally hidden by shelving and sacks of coal. Cramming bags of food and bottles of water inside as quickly as she could, she immediately slammed it shut again, her heart pounding in her narrow ribcage, half-expecting the creatures to come flying out at her through the concrete.

Even after she'd locked up and returned home it took her hours to stop trembling. Never again, she told herself. From then on she came to the house only to feed the dogs, trying hard to bury the thought of the two small girls entombed without food or water in the darkness below.

It wasn't until late March 1996 that Marc Dutroux was released from prison. One of the first things he did was to head straight for his house in Marcinelle. What went through his mind as he made his way down to the basement he'd 'renovated' so proudly? Did he listen through the wall for the sound of children's voices and take a deep breath before he prised the door open, already half-afraid of what he was going to find?

All we can be certain of is that when Marc Dutroux crawled inside the concealed dungeon he'd made, he found inside the emaciated bodies of two little girls, each weighing little over two stone. Both were dead.

'I told you to feed them!' he yelled at Michelle, more furious that his orders had been disobeyed than that his helpless prisoners had lost their lives. In a rage, he wrapped the frail bodies in plastic bin liners and carried them to the big deep freeze. They were so light, lifting them inside took no more effort than sticking in a couple of frozen chickens.

Once the freezer door was safely shut, he set about cleaning up the house. The dogs had been there, more or less alone for four months, and the place was full of dog excrement and the foul stench caught on your nostrils as soon as you walked in. Damn Michelle, he thought angrily. The only things she'd had to do and she'd completely messed up!

It was another week before the bodies of Julie and Melissa were taken out of the freezer and buried in the garden of another of his houses, alongside Weinstein in their plastic bin-liner shrouds. Now Dutroux was restless. He'd thought about the children all the time he was in prison, and now they were dead, the dungeon lying empty and unused. He needed to go out and procure some more girls.

On 28 May 1996, Sabine Dardenne strapped her satchel to her back and set off for school as normal on her bike from her home in the town of Kain, waving to her father as she rode off.

This would be the last time that he would see his daughter for two and a half months. And when she did return again, the 12-year-old, with her curly blonde hair and clumsy unguarded grin, would be someone different, someone who rarely smiled, and who shrank from her own father's touch.

Just moments after setting off, a beaten-up old camper van pulled up alongside Sabine. The sliding door opened and she was pulled from her bike into the moving vehicle. With a blanket over her head, Sabine couldn't see what was happening, or who had taken her, but she knew enough to be terrified for her life. After being drugged and trussed up inside an old rusty trunk, she was taken to the secret dungeon, where just months before, two little girls had slowly starved to death.

Sabine would spend seventy-nine harrowing days there, naked and chained by the neck, used and abused by Marc Dutroux, forced to take part in pornographic films made for men willing to pay big money to see children crying in pain, pleading for help from the very adults brutalising them.

Quite apart from the sexual torture, Marc Dutroux took perverse pleasure in playing sick psychological games with the traumatised girl. He told her that her parents knew exactly where she was, but that they didn't want to pay for her release. As with Eefje and An, Sabine was assured there were bad people out there who would kill her if they got hold of her, but that he, Marc, was trying to protect her.

'They're constantly watching the house,' he warned her. 'If you try to escape, they'll kill you instantly.'

Michelle Martin, the former teacher and now a mother of three, was nowhere to be seen. After a few days of captivity, Sabine was told her parents considered her as good as dead and had already packed her things up in boxes. In the absence of an adult in whom to confide, Sabine was forced to turn for help and comfort to the very man who had introduced her to this living hell: Marc Dutroux.

In the secret diary Sabine kept, days were marked with either a star or a cross. The star days were when Marc came to see her and just chatted, as if he were a friendly uncle or caring teacher. The cross days were the ones when he raped her. Occasionally the lines between abuser and saviour became very blurred, as when Dutroux would force her to perform oral sex and then offer her sweets 'to take the taste away', as if he'd just been giving her foul-tasting medicine for her own good.

The lonely, traumatised girl wrote endless letters to her mother, telling her about the 'agony room', as she'd renamed the dungeon, about how she wished they'd come for her. With heartbreaking poignancy, she'd ask after her friends, her sisters, as if by talking about normal things somehow she might be able to will herself back there, in the parallel universe she'd once inhabited, where children got up in the morning and went to school unmolested, and the worst thing they had to worry about was arguing with their parents over chores or homework.

When Dutroux would tell her that her mum had replied, instructing her to let him have sex with her, Sabine wondered whether she was being punished, whether her mum doubted that she loved her.

'If I didn't love you, why would I go to the bakery for you and iron handkerchiefs?' she wrote sadly.

And where was Michelle Martin while all this was going on? Did she ever look at her own children as they sat around the dinner table, tucking into a hot meal, and think of the young girl alone in the dungeon, eating cold tinned food in the dark, or the two others who'd wasted away because she was too nervous to feed them? And did she ever kiss the top of her son's head, breathing in the smell of soap and freshly washed hair and wonder about those other mothers, the ones whose children went out one day and never came back?

Probably not, because by this stage Michelle had forgotten what it was like to feel empathy for someone else. She'd cohabited so long with brutality that it was the only master she knew. As always, she turned her narrow back, and did nothing.

Meanwhile, Sabine was desperately lonely in her underground prison.

'Do you think one of my friends could come round and visit me?' she asked her captor, still not really understanding what had happened to her.

Marc Dutroux's response was to kidnap another girl. Not only would he have a new sexual plaything – another star for his sickening pornographic videos – it would also give Sabine yet another reason to feel grateful to him.

On 9 August 1996, 14-year-old Laetitia Delhez went swimming at a pool in her home town: Bertrix in the south-east of Belgium. As she walked home, a shabby white van pulled up alongside her. No one heard her scream.

'I have a friend for you!'

Marc Dutroux pushed the terrified Laetitia ahead of him into the filthy dungeon, which Sabine now called home. The girls locked eyes in mutual helpless appeal. Now Sabine was torn between relief at having someone to talk to, and guilt that it was her fault Laetitia was there.

If Dutroux's intention had been to add an extra layer of psychological torture for his poor captive, he couldn't have planned it better. But this time he made one fateful error. While he and Lelièvre had been driving around Bertrix looking for potential victims they'd been spotted by a student who thought there was something odd about the battered van that was covered in stickers. When police trawled the area searching for witnesses, the young man was able to tell them the exact make of the van and even the first part of the number plate which had stuck in his mind because it had the same initials as his sister.

Jean-Marc Connerotte, the magistrate in charge of the Bertrix area, ordered Marc Dutroux's arrest. He also had all his houses surrounded.

After two days of intense questioning, Dutroux finally cracked. 'I'll give you some girls,' he told the incredulous police officers.

It was an apprehensive group who accompanied Dutroux to his house in Marcinelle on 15 August 1996. Smashing through the concrete behind the filing cabinet, which now hid the door to the cellar, the men were horrified to find two emaciated young girls, who cowered and cried at their sudden appearance. Believing these were the bad guys who had sworn to kill them, the girls ran for comfort to the familiar figure of Dutroux.

'Thank you,' they sobbed, clinging to the man they believed, in spite of the rapes, the videotaping, the long nights spent chained to him by the foot, had protected them.

For magistrate Jean-Marc Connerotte this was the most heartrending sight of all.

In the eight long years following the arrest of Marc Dutroux and Michelle Martin, Belgium tore its public heart out over the man who became known as The Beast of Belgium. Why hadn't Dutroux been stopped earlier? And why had the police investigation been so inept? Then, again and again, the question of the day: were Dutroux and Martin and Lelièvre acting alone?

From the start, Marc Dutroux insisted he'd kidnapped the girls to order for an international paedophile ring which boasted members from the very highest levels of Belgian society, including police officers, government officials, even members of the Royal Family. One of the men who would later stand trial with him was Michel Nihoul, a fraudster rumoured to organise sex and drugs parties for Belgium's elite. Dutroux accused Nihoul of being his link to an organised crime ring that stole girls to order and then sold them into prostitution in other parts of Europe.

Certainly, there was a lot of evidence to support his claim. Despite numerous warning signs, police had been suspiciously slow to react, and subsequently, calamitously inept. Following his arrest, crucial evidence, such as analysis of hair samples taken from the dungeon, was dismissed or discarded. Connerotte, who'd cracked open the case and who many Belgians believed to be one of the few totally independent authority figures, was removed from the investigation. The official reason given was that he had attended a fund-raising event in October 1996 at which some of the families of Dutroux' victims were present, and had so compromised his impartiality. Witnesses who came forward to testify to the existence of a highly organised paedophile ring, in which children were tortured and in some cases even murdered at parties, were discredited. Several other witnesses died unexpectedly before they could give evidence, yet still Dutroux mouldered in jail, and still there was no trial, no closure.

Finally, in June 2004, a court at Arlon in eastern Belgium tried Dutroux for rape, kidnap and murder. His wife, Nihoul and Lelièvre were also in the dock as accomplices. Like the rest of Belgium, the families of the victims were divided – some came to the court to see justice done, others stayed away, convinced the real perpetrators were still at large and protected.

By this stage Michelle Martin was divorced from her controlling former husband. In the dock, she seemed to shrink away from him, as insubstantial in the flesh as she was in spirit. She was a hollow woman whose blind self-interest had allowed two children to die and a sadist to live out his fantasies unchallenged.

But Michelle attempted to somehow justify herself. She had been terrified of her husband and she was frightened of the girls in the cellar.

'I thought the little creatures would attack me,' she told the hushed court.

Of course she should have let them out, should have protected Sabine and Laetitia, but she didn't.

'I want to express my regrets,' she said lamely, facing the two survivors of the dungeon across the courtroom. For them it was too little, far, far too late.

Her husband too made a half-hearted attempt at a remorse hardly anyone believed him capable of.

'I realise the wrong that I have done,' he said. 'I offer my apologies.'

They were not accepted.

After a trial which half of Belgium believed to be an official whitewash, Marc Dutroux was imprisoned for life for the murder of Eefje, An and Bernard Weinstein. Michelle Martin received thirty years for allowing two little girls to starve to death in a cellar. Lelièvre, who'd accompanied Dutroux on his kidnapping expeditions, was jailed for twenty-five years, while Nihoul, widely rumoured to have been the lynchpin in an international crime ring dealing in abduction, pornography and human trafficking, got off with a five-year sentence for drug dealing and fraud.

The trial and sentences did little to heal the broken heart of Belgium, where even today, question marks still hang heavy over the narrow focus of the investigation and the staggering ineptitude of the police. Claims of sex parties, in which the ruling elite got drunk on watching children being tortured, seem as incredible now as they did when they were first mooted and yet, can anything really be beyond belief in a world where 8-year-olds can be snatched from the street and starved to death in underground dungeons?

Whether he worked alone, or as he claims as a 'lowly cog in a sex slave ring', the fact remains that Marc Dutroux was a sadist and a psychopath, chilling in his brutality, more chilling still in his attempts to befriend his victims, to extract gratitude instead of fear. Michelle Martin was a weak woman who literally stood by her man, even when he was raping children, who became so much of a moral void that she allowed two 8-year-olds to die with the same lack of conscience as if they were a couple of rabid dogs she feared would attack her if she approached.

Marc Dutroux's mother told authorities that her son was born with a 'twisted soul'. The pity is how easily he managed to twist his wife's soul to match his own, and with such devastating results.

## CHAPTER 9

# BULLY FOR LOVE

## DIARY OF A DEATH

### AMANDA BAGGUS AND DAVID LEHANE

Sitting at the table in her home in Bream in the peaceful Forest of Dean, nestling amid the rolling Gloucestershire countryside, Amanda Baggus chewed the end of her biro as she considered where to start. The diary was open in front of her, page after page of lined, spiral-bound paper, filled with her neat round, child-like writing. She'd already written the date at the top of the blank page: 5-08-06, just as she'd learned to do while doing homework at school. After a few moments of thought, she took the pen out of her mouth and began to write.

But Amanda wasn't writing about what had happened to her that day, nor was she keeping a note of her son's milestone achievements, or even jotting down her hopes and dreams for the future. No, the 25-year-old's diary was altogether far more disturbing. In childish writing littered with misspellings that made the contrast to the blood-chilling content even more stark, Amanda was chronicling the systematic abuse and torture of the man she and her boyfriend were keeping prisoner in their garden shed, the man they simply called 'prick'.

'He was playing up late nite banging in the shed,' she wrote, the tip of her tongue protruding slightly, as she concentrated on the task in hand. 'So later that nite both Scott and Dave hit Prick until quite late cause Prick made a load of shouting. Hoovered three times.'

According to her diary, Amanda did a lot of hoovering: hoovering to clean away the evidence of their systematic brutality, hoovering to cover the sound of a man howling with pain and pleading for his life… But there are some stains that no amount of cleaning will ever expunge, some sounds that linger on long after the event.

And there are some diaries that should never be written.

'You idiot! What did you go and do that for? Now look what's happened!'

Amanda Baggus was fuming, her face puce with anger as she surveyed the damage to her Reliant Robin, which lay on its side in the road.

'I'm sorry, Amanda. I didn't mean to, honest.'

Always inclined to trip over his words, Kevin Davies' nerves now made him almost incoherent.

He hadn't a clue that the little three-wheeler car might topple over if he opened his door while it was still moving, and to be completely honest he wasn't even sure it was definitely his fault, but one look at Amanda's face told him he was in big trouble.

'You're going to pay for this,' she spat, her face, distorted with rage, pressed up close to his.

As a dismayed Kevin cast an eye over the beaten-up old car that day in May 2006, trying desperately to work out how much it would cost to put right, he had no idea that the price he'd end up paying for his 'mistake' would be his life.

Later that day, Amanda was still seething when she recounted the incident to her boyfriend of ten years, David Lehane.

'It's the last straw, Dave,' she ranted. 'If that prick thinks he can wreck my car and just walk away scot-free, he's got another thing coming!'

David listened, his close-set green eyes glinting in his hard, narrow face. The 35-year-old had known Kevin Davies since school days and had even let him help him out with one or other of his business ventures from time to time, but recently he'd become a real pain. Since his epilepsy had got too bad for him to work, Kevin had taken to just hanging around the couple and he was getting on their nerves. Sometimes they let him stick around in return for him buying them drinks and things such as takeaway meals, but now look what had happened.

'You're right, he's got some serious damage to put right,' he mused. 'Shame he's got no money.'

'No, but he's got his benefit,' Amanda reminded him.

A plan was slowly beginning to form in her mind.

Bream, in the Forest of Dean, is one of those places that perfectly epitomises William Blake's 'England's green and promised land'. A large self-contained village with plenty of green spaces for children to play and surrounded on all sides by rolling hills and woodland, Bream is the kind of place where young parents dream of bringing up their families and pensioners grow old without fear.

The neat semi-detached house in which David Lehane and Amanda Baggus lived was situated at one end of a quiet cul-de-sac with a well-kept garden to the back and side. Even though it was a housing association property, it was the envy of many of their friends, and the couple looked after it well. It was a shame really that their son was being looked after by relatives rather than living with them – this would have made a perfect family home.

The only thing that slightly let the house down was the makeshift shed in the back garden. This was a ramshackle structure, tucked away round one side of the house, between the wall of the back extension and the red brick wall that separated the house from its neighbours. Whoever had built the shed had obviously done so in rather a hurry. A wooden door with frosted glass panels, of the type you normally find on a back kitchen, had been carelessly joined onto a basic four-walled cube of corrugated iron, finished off on the roof with four lengths of plastic drain pipe, cut in halves and placed upside down. Two large metal bolts had been firmly hammered onto the outside of the door. Inside, off-cuts of laminated wood panels had been laid randomly down on the floor and a few tiles stuck to the wall. Measuring around 6 by 4ft, this was the sort of structure that an enthusiastic teenager, just experimenting with carpentry, might just cobble together to impress his indulgent mother.

It was to be Kevin Davies' home for the last four agonising months of his life.

At first it had just been a business proposition: they'd keep Kevin prisoner in the shed, cashing in his benefits, until they reckoned he'd repaid his debt for the damage to the car. If they made him hand back the keys to his housing association flat, they could pretend he was living with them and claim rent too.

It wasn't as if they really needed the money either. David Lehane had claimed benefits ever since an attack of psoriasis some years before, but that hadn't stopped him from running a car repairs business and a landscape gardening service on the side. The money wasn't really the point, though. Amanda Baggus, small-minded and vindictive, wanted to see Kevin Davies punished for what he'd done to her car. And, with the sadistic mentality that had made her the class bully at school, she thought it would be fun to see the weak, placid man squirm a bit and to remind him who was boss around there.

'Come on, let's do it,' she urged Lehane.

He didn't need much encouragement.

Kevin Davies, a severe epileptic for the past fifteen years, had always had a problem forming close friendships. Softly spoken and passive by nature, he was well liked around the close-knit community where he grew up, but preferred to eschew group situations in favour of his own company.

He was close to his mother and family, but when the council had re-housed him to Bream, a few miles away, he'd become even more solitary in his habits. In recent years he'd started drinking a fair bit, but he was never an aggressive drunk as so many seemed to be. Sometimes he'd get drunk alone, and other times with one of his few local friends, like David Lehane.

Amanda Baggus knew it would be a while before he was missed. In the meantime, they could have some fun.

As soon as the Robin Reliant was damaged, Kevin had worried about what David Lehane's reaction might be, but even so it didn't occur to him that he was in any real danger. True, David had a reputation for violence. On more than a few occasions, Kevin had been on the receiving end of Lehane's fist and had had to hand over money to him and his girlfriend from time to time. But still 29-year-old Kevin didn't think he'd ever really hurt him. After all, he'd known David for years.

'I'm really sorry about the car,' Kevin repeated for the hundredth time. 'I'll pay you back. Really.'

'Too right you will!' Lehane was leading Kevin round the side of the house to the dark patch of muddy grass that housed the DIY shed.

'Say hello to your new home.'

Alone in the shed, Kevin listened uncomprehendingly to the noise of the bolts being drawn across the door from the outside. He didn't understand. Why was he here? What was going on?

'David,' he called tentatively. 'Amanda…'

No one answered.

'Did you see his face?' David was laughing. 'He didn't have a clue what was going on.'

In truth it had been so easy. And now they had a man imprisoned in their garden shed, completely at their mercy. It was an empowering idea.

The violence started soon after Kevin was first incarcerated. Amanda just couldn't bear the noises he was making – shouting and banging things on the side of the shed.

'He's got to be taught a lesson,' she decided. 'He's got to learn to shut up.'

The girl who'd terrorised classmates at school was an old hand at teaching people to keep quiet. Kevin's 'lesson' involved being hit over the head with a wooden bar.

Kevin Davies, crouching alone and terrified in a corner of the shed clutched his bleeding head and whimpered softly to himself. What was happening to him didn't seem possible. They were bound to release him in a day or two, he tried to reassure himself; they'd warn him not to tell anyone and send him home, he thought.

But the couple weren't about to stop there. That initial beating had given them a thrill way beyond the original intent of teaching their prisoner a lesson. They discovered they liked administering punishment; they enjoyed the way fear flared up in Kevin's wide, trusting green eyes. It was similar to when they'd picked on younger, weaker kids at school, only this time there was no teacher to tell them to pack it in, no angry parent waiting at the school gates. There really were no limits.

'He's been at it again,' Amanda would tell her boyfriend, her round face lit up with anticipation. 'You'd better do something.'

Then Dave would go to the shed and use his fists, or the wooden bar. Amanda would either go to watch, or listen to the muffled cries coming through the door.

'Good job she's so deaf,' she said, when David reappeared, gesturing towards the neighbouring house, where 84-year-old Esme Palmer pottered in her kitchen, blissfully unaware of what was happening just yards away.

The couple started to bring Kevin into the house – except that now he'd become their prisoner, and therefore in their eyes something less than human, so they no longer called him by his name. Instead they referred to him as 'Prick'. In the relative privacy of their living room, they could pile more abuse onto their helpless captive, secure that his screams wouldn't be overheard.

'I can't find an ashtray, come over here, Kevin,' Amanda would say, stubbing her cigarette out on her former friend's bare skin.

'He kept me awake again last night,' she'd complain to her boyfriend. 'You'd better do something.'

And she'd watch, grinning, as Kevin was beaten, kicked and stamped on. Or else she'd join in with the abuse. They liked to make him strip, enjoying his shame and humiliation.

'Oh, sorry, did that get on you?' one or other would leer as they poured scalding water over his exposed genitals and thighs.

Every week Kevin's benefit cheque would go straight into the couple's pockets, helping to keep them in expensive clothes, CDs and alcohol, which they drank throughout the day. Keeping Kevin had become both a financial investment and a blood sport.

Even when Amanda and David took in a new lodger – a friend of theirs called Scott Andrews – the abuse didn't stop. In fact, with a third fit, strong adult around to help out, the beatings intensified. Knowing his 'friends' and landlords believed Kevin to be less than human, Andrews, taking his cue from them, came to regard the man in the shed as little more than a useless dog in need of discipline.

During the daytime, Kevin was put to work in the house: vacuuming, washing up and cleaning up after his captors. At night he shivered in the unheated shed, trying to muffle his sobs so he wouldn't get punished the next day for keeping his captors awake. Fed only on potato peelings and scraps of leftovers his 6ft 2 frame gradually wasted away to skeletal proportions.

Of course his family, to whom he was close, were concerned when he stopped coming to see them. But his captors made sure they didn't come round to check on him by forcing Kevin to phone his mum, Elizabeth James, to say he was OK.

'I'm fine, Mum,' he said stiltedly, knowing he'd get the beating of his life if he let slip anything about what was really going on. 'I've given up my flat, but I'm living with friends.'

But his voice sounded flat and thin. Elizabeth instinctively felt something was not quite right. Was he taking his epilepsy medicine? Was he eating properly? She called 1471 trying to trace the number, but there was no record.

'He's 29, you know. He's a grown up,' friends told her, when she said she was worried. She supposed they were right.

Meanwhile, Kevin's existence was getting more miserable every day. His three tormentors, largely bored and under-occupied, amused themselves by coming up with ever more extreme and imaginative ways to make his life hell.

One day they marched him barefoot into the house and ordered him to get down on the floor. He sat with his back to the wall, hugging his emaciated arms around his hollow chest, trying to stop himself from shaking. His head had been shaved and the contours of his skull showed clearly through his painfully stretched scalp. His thin T-shirt looked baggy and enormous in contrast to his scrawny neck and emaciated frame. Without any fat to protect them, his protruding bones hurt where they came into contact with the floor.

Kevin's eyes, huge in his skull-like face, gazed up at his captors with a wary apprehension. What were they planning now? Why were they getting out that video camera? All too soon, their intention became clear. Inspired by the grainy hostage videos they saw coming out of Iraq on the nightly news, Amanda, David and Scott had decided to make one of their own.

'Speak, speak!'

Kevin, conscious of the whirring of the camera, tried to remember the script he'd just been told to say. He mumbled something about being kept for his own safety.

'Are you being nicely fed?'

The question was like some sick joke. Kevin couldn't

remember the last time he'd had a proper meal and hadn't gone to sleep with the sound of his own hunger growling in his ears.

'I'm being fed perfectly, actually,' he lied, his arms instinctively crossing over his concave abdomen. If he said the right thing, they might be happy with him and not hurt him today. He had to try to think of something that would please them.

'I have been previously enjoying it,' he ventured, as if he were describing a stay in a holiday camp. 'It's very good.'

Amanda Baggus tried to smother her giggles as she watched 'Prick' struggling with his words. It was so funny, hearing him thanking them for everything they'd done for him. He really was pathetic. She just hoped he wouldn't soil her carpet – there was a sour, decaying smell about him that made her cringe.

Summer would normally have been Kevin Davies' favourite time of year. A nature lover, he'd be gone for hours, days even, walking in the beautiful Forest of Dean countryside with one of the various dogs he'd kept over the years. But the summer of 2006 was different. The few snatched seconds where he was shuttled between shed and house were the only time Kevin saw the sun. Sometimes, when he'd been locked up in the darkness for a particularly long time, the sudden daylight when the shed door was opened would be practically blinding and he'd blink upwards, squinting in fear at whichever of his three prison guards stood in the doorway, silhouetted against the impossibly blue sky.

As June dissolved into July and then August, Kevin could only dream about heading out into the cool forests, where a person might walk for hours and never come across another soul, just surrender himself to the beauty of nature, allow himself to be carried on the breeze like a leaf from a tree, each journey becoming an adventure.

And then the summer was gone, passed in a blur; like scenery glimpsed from a moving train, forever out of reach. September arrived and the streets of Bream were once again filled with children, bags slung low over shoulders, heading off to a new school year.

And still Kevin's nightmare wasn't over. Still the relentless cycle of chores, beatings and slow systematic starvation continued. He grew ever weaker, ever thinner.

'Get up! What are you doing?' The harsh, shrill voice held an edge of panic as Amanda Baggus gazed in horror at the prone figure on the kitchen floor.

It was late in the evening on 26 September and 'Prick' had been allowed into the house, but all of a sudden he had fallen to the floor and now she couldn't get him to stand up. She couldn't even tell if he was breathing.

Waiting for the ambulance to arrive, they came up with a story. Kevin had turned up at the house earlier that evening, asking if he could stay the night. Then he'd collapsed on the floor. Everyone knew he had a history of epilepsy – no one would question that he'd fallen while suffering a seizure.

By that stage, the three were so deeply entrenched in their own twisted reality, where they were the bosses and the man in the shed didn't really exist as a human being – just a name on a benefit cheque, a dog that needed whipping – that they didn't think of how the scene would look to outsiders. A 6ft 2 man, weighing just 7 stone, his bones pressing through his pale, light-starved skin like groceries in an overstuffed shopping bag, his body covered in burns and bruises...

When Kevin was declared dead, police officers came to search the house in which he'd died, their minds unable to shake off the image of the cross seared into his buttocks, or the scars from where scalding liquid had been thrown over his skin.

'I think I've got something,' said an officer. The camcorder, with its damning hostage film, was wrapped in plastic and removed from the house; ditto Amanda Baggus' diary, gleefully detailing each new atrocity in her neat schoolgirl writing. Spatters of blood were found on the ceiling, walls and furniture of the house and in the shed that, for the last months of his life, had been the only home Kevin knew. The kidnapping that had lasted for months in the very midst of a gentile, close-knit English community was finally at an end.

In July 2007, Amanda Baggus and David Lehane were jailed for ten years and Scott Andrews for nine, after being found guilty of assault and false imprisonment. To the outrage of many, particularly Kevin's heartbroken mother, murder charges had to be dropped as it was impossible to prove Kevin's epilepsy hadn't contributed to his death.

There will always be bullies in this world, people who get a thrill from inflicting misery on others weaker than them. The tragedy of Kevin Davies is that he came into contact with a couple whose bullying natures had first brought them together, who reinforced one another's warped view of a world which had themselves at the centre. Anyone weaker became fair game.

'I can't believe anyone would be so cruel,' said Elizabeth James, after the trial of her son's persecutors.

The truth of it was that Amanda Baggus and David Lehane didn't believe what they were doing was cruel. They thought it was fun. Isolated, bullies are destructive. In pairs, they can be deadly.

# 'GO ON, JUMP!'

## SARAH BULLOCK AND DARREN STEWART

'Go on, JUMP!'

He was tired, so tired. His legs felt like they'd been weighted down by concrete blocks. Each step was a test of endurance, like wading through PVA glue. And still they climbed higher and higher.

'I can't go on any more.' The sob ripped from his throat like a razor blade.

'You have to, Steve. Otherwise the snipers will get you. They're hiding in the bushes, you know, just waiting for you to slow down.'

Fearfully, he looked over into the dark shadows where men he didn't know were waiting to shoot him. There, that faint rustling of leaves. Was that one of them, trying to get a better position so he could take aim?

'Come on, Steve. We're nearly there.'

The others seemed to be finding something funny, but he couldn't for the life of him imagine what it might be. They were behind him, giggling. Every now and then when his legs grew too heavy, one of them would give him a shove to jumpstart him into moving again.

Why was he so tired? Why did everything feel so strange? He just wanted to go home again.

'I don't want to go there.' He was gazing in horror ahead, where the path led onto a viaduct, with 100ft drops on either side. 'It's too high. Don't make me go there!'

Their voices were bubbling with barely suppressed laughter.

'You *have* to keep going, Steve. You don't want to be shot, do you?' they said.

Legs trembling, he edged out along the viaduct, trying not to look down to where the town of St Austell lay in the darkness like a miniature model village, the sea an inky expanse in the distance. He was just so tired.

Finally they stopped. He clung onto the railing, hoping it would stop his shaking legs from buckling under him.

'Now climb over.'

Through his exhaustion he heard the command as if it had come from a long way off. He struggled to make sense of it. Why did they want him to climb over this railing when it was so high up? He was too tired – he just wanted to go home.

'Climb over – or they'll shoot you.'

Terrified, he peered behind him into the shadows. He was

sure he could hear people moving, the sounds of gun barrels being clicked.

Whimpering with fear, he began to climb over the safety rail. He was trembling so much that he could hardly force his limbs to move. On the other side, he hung onto the top rail and tried to wedge his feet under the bottom one, but that wasn't allowed.

'You have to hang down from the railings,' they told him. 'It's your only chance.'

He was now so tired that he'd stopped trying to make sense of it. All he knew was that he was being given commands, and he had to obey or something terrible would happen to him. Sobbing openly now, he crouched down and moved his hands lower down the rails. And then he was hanging there, his legs dangling over the sheer drop. Only his hands gripping the rail, palms slippery with sweat, prevented him from falling into the terrifying abyss below.

And then the girl stepped forward. Maybe she's coming to help me, thought the exhausted man, hope rising suddenly above the fear. She had a smile on her face, as though she was sharing a joke she was about to let him in on. But instead of extending a helping hand, she raised up her leg and brought her foot crashing down on his knuckles… again and again…

'Come on, you prick, jump!' she jeered.

And then everything went black.

Steven Hoskin was thrilled when he got the keys to what would be his first-ever home of his own. OK, it was only a housing association bedsit, but for the 39-year-old man who suffered severe learning difficulties, this was a major breakthrough in independence.

Situated in the Cornish market town of St Austell, in a quiet residential close, the tiny flat was a huge step forwards for Steven, who'd lived with his mum until she became too ill, just a couple of years before, and had been in and out of temporary accommodation ever since. Here, he'd be able to unpack properly, to make a real home for his beloved pet terrier dog, perhaps even make a few friends.

Steven had grown up in the nearby village of Maudlin, near Bodmin. Although he'd found school an ordeal, his easy-going nature had made him a well-liked figure around the closely-knit village. Local people realised he was essentially a child trapped in an adult's body, and they watched out for him, making sure no one took advantage of him. The move to St Austell would take him well out of his comfort zone. Would he be able to meet people he liked there, away from his familiar support network?

When he first moved into Blowing House Close in the spring of 2005, Steven was understandably nervous. St Austell isn't a huge town. Bordered on one side by the sea and on the other by the towering arches of the Trenance Viaduct, built by the Great Western Railway in 1898, these days its main claim to fame is being the closest point to the Eden Project, situated just a couple of miles away. But to Steven, who was used to living in a small village where everyone knew who he was, it might as well have been New York City.

He spent ages gazing out of his window at the street corner below, where he always saw the same young man hanging around. This man was hardly ever alone. As he stood there, he'd be joined first by one group of youngsters, then another. For lonely Steven, that convivial corner looked like a charmed place so he was thrilled when, one day, the man on the corner started chatting to him.

'Guess what?' he proudly announced to his friends back in Maudlin the next time he spoke to them on the phone. 'I'm in a gang!'

To Steven's amazement, the man on the corner, Darren Stewart, had taken a real interest in him. He'd been keen to find out exactly where he lived and had even started to invite all his friends round to Steven's flat. From being a quiet, rather lonely place, the little bedsit was suddenly filled with people all through the day and night. To Steven, desperate to feel he belonged, it was a dream come true.

'Can't you keep the noise down? How many times do we have to come round here?'

Steven didn't like it when his neighbours came to the door to complain about the loud music and the sound of people coming and going all through the night. But he couldn't tell them to leave, could he? They were his friends. He didn't want to be on his own again.

Secretly though, he was a bit nervous of some of the people who came round. Steven wasn't worldly by a long stretch of the imagination, but even he knew enough to see that there was a lot of alcohol going round at these impromptu 'parties', and lots of 'other stuff' too.

In reality, 30-year-old Darren (Daz) Stewart was turning Steven Hoskin's flat into his own private party venue – a convenient pad where he could supply alcohol and, rumour had it, drugs to the neighbourhood's teenagers, a place where he and his girlfriend Sarah could get all their mates round and have a laugh.

Sarah Bullock was just 16 and completely in thrall to her new lover. To her immature mind, Daz Stewart was the epitome of the cool, sophisticated older man. He knew everyone and always seemed to have a regular stash of amphetamines to hand. And now he'd found them this flat so they no longer had to hang around street corners. Yeah, it was a shame about the loser who lived there, who was always hanging about, but that was just something they had to put up with. Anyway, he had his uses – he was gullible enough to hand over his benefit money without a word.

Within months of moving into Blowing House Close, Steven Hoskin had a new flatmate: Darren Stewart had moved in. But if Steven had been envisaging friendly chats in front of the TV or companionable meals for two, he was much mistaken.

'You must have some more money. Hand it over, or you know what's coming to you!' Daz Stewart knew exactly which tone of voice scared his new flatmate the most. A bully by nature, he enjoyed seeing the fear in Steve Hoskin's trusting brown eyes as he scurried around, looking for any money he may have overlooked.

Really, Daz thought contentedly, this was working out better than he could have expected. He now had a base of operations, somewhere to bring his mates and a ready source of income. All he had to do was keep plying Steve with alcohol, put the frighteners on him every now and then, and he was good as gold. Besides, he was proving very useful for some things.

'Oi, get me another drink!'

Sarah was lying on the sofa with her head in Darren's lap, waving her empty beer can around.

Wearily, Steve hauled himself up and made his way to the little kitchen to fetch another can from the fridge. He didn't like the way Sarah and Daz talked to him now, but he didn't know what he could do about it. He didn't want to go back to being lonely again, and he was also scared of what they might do to him. They were always pushing him about and hurting him, but he didn't know how to make it stop.

Every week when his social worker came to see him, he just said everything was OK. He didn't want to get his friends into trouble: he was a grown-up now – he could manage.

Neighbours' complaints about the noise coming from Steven's flat fell on deaf ears. Sarah Bullock's mum and stepfather started to hear rumours about what was going on and tried to persuade her to stop seeing Darren Stewart. He was so much older, they were sure he was getting her involved in all sorts of trouble... You only had to look at her pasty complexion and lank hair to know that it wasn't vitamin pills she was popping those nights when she didn't come home.

'Yeah, well, you can't tell me what to do,' Sarah sneered at them, hardly recognisable as the smiling young girl in her school photos just a few short years before. 'Anyway, I'm moving in with Daz.'

Despite their objections, Darren Stewart turned up at the door to pick up Sarah's things, laughing in the face of her parents' protestations. And then the two of them were gone.

Now Steven Hoskin had two flatmates – and his life was about to descend into hell.

The combination of bullies and boredom is always an explosive one, and Darren and Sarah, with long empty days and nights stretching ahead of them, amused themselves by inventing a new game: torturing Steve.

'Sorry, did that burn you?' they'd laugh, as Steven whelped with pain, rubbing his arm where a cigarette had just been stubbed out on his skin. Other friends who came to the flat to take advantage of Steven's hospitality also joined in the new sport.

'Come here and lick this up,' they'd order their host, forcing him down on his hands and knees next to a puddle of spilled drink.

Humiliated, scared and uncomprehending, Steven would put his face to the ground and tentatively put his tongue out towards the puddle of liquid.

'Look at him,' his guests would scoff. 'Licking the floor like a dog!'

That gave Sarah an idea. Bending down to Steven's pet terrier, she unbuckled its collar and then she reached up and secured it around Steven's neck. Hardly able to speak for laughing, she picked up the little creature's lead.

'Walkies!' she cried, clipping it onto the collar around Steven's neck. And, to snorts of derision from the assembled hangers-on, she began pulling her host around the room. 'Fetch!' she ordered him. 'Beg!'

'Please, Madam,' Steve obliged wretchedly, earning himself a roar of laughter from the assembled company. He'd learned long ago to be sure to address Darren as 'Sir' and to call Sarah 'Madam'.

He was miserable, but he didn't know what to do. They were the only friends he had there and he was completely terrified of them. When Darren told him to tell his social worker that he didn't want to see anyone from the social services department any more, he complied. By this stage he'd do anything to avoid another beating.

Sarah Bullock's mother too had been in touch with social services, anxious to see what could be done about her increasingly distant daughter. She also called the police: 'Can't you just go in there and arrest her for anything? I don't care what it is, just as long as she gets away from Darren Stewart!'

But nothing was done.

Wednesday, 5 July 2006 was another long, aimless day for the occupants of Blowing House Close. Time hangs heavily on your hands when you're sitting in a tiny, cramped room, where the summer sun barely filters through the cloud of cigarette smoke in the alcohol-soaked air. By the time night fell, they were restless and looking for some entertainment.

'See him, he's a paedophile, he is,' Darren was talking to his friend Martin Pollard and gesturing his head towards a nervous-looking Steve. 'Aren't you? Admit it, you're a paedophile.'

Steven Hoskin, whose IQ ranked him in the bottom half per cent of the population, didn't even know what a paedophile was.

Now Sarah Bullock was catching onto the game.

'Go on, admit it,' she said, advancing menacingly towards Steven. 'Admit you're a nonce!'

And so began the final, most harrowing part of the game that started with boredom and ended in murder: over the course of that evening, Steven Hoskin was beaten and tortured like never before. Forced under duress to confess to being a paedophile, he was then made to sit against the wall under graffiti spelling out messages such as 'should be hung' and 'scum'.

Martin Pollard really did believe Sarah and Darren's lies about their host. As the alcohol flowed what started out as a bit of fun was deadly serious.

'Paedophiles like you are disgusting – you don't deserve to live!'

Who was it who said that? No matter. The little court of three was quick to agree: Steven Hoskin should die.

'Here, swallow these. Come on, do it!'

Steven, by now in terrible pain and terrified of what was going to happen, looked in confusion at the handful of white pills he was being offered.

'I… I don't want to…'

'Who cares what you want, just swallow them!'

Whimpering softly, Steven began to swallow the paracetamol tablets one by one, gagging as he forced them down his dry throat. Fifty pills. Sixty. And still they kept coming.

When he'd taken about seventy pills, the helpless man

was frog-marched through the door of the flat out into the July night.

'Where are we going?' he asked, wonderingly as the group headed towards the viaduct at the top of the town. 'I don't want to go up there!'

In truth Steven was terrified of heights, a fact his tormentors knew very well.

'Keep moving and don't make a sound,' they warned him, knowing only too well how gullible he was. 'There are snipers everywhere and they'll shoot you if they hear you.'

A vulnerable, terrified man, his body sluggish with painkillers, was made to walk up to a viaduct and climb over the railings, his legs dangling thirty metres above the town. Then a 16-year-old girl, high on power, stamped on his hands where they gripped onto the bars, his knuckles white and straining with the effort of clinging on.

Steven Hoskin plummeted to the ground, his body slamming down onto the roof of a car parked underneath. He died instantly.

Afterwards, Sarah Bullock and Darren Stewart returned to the flat, still exhilarated by what they'd just done.

Darren wanted to tidy the place up, but his young girlfriend had other ideas.

'Let's have a bit of playtime,' she said suggestively. 'Come on, I want to play.'

So they had sex in the very flat where just hours before they'd sentenced an innocent man to death, under walls still dripping with painted messages of hate.

At their trial exactly one year later, Darren Stewart and Sarah Bullock were both found guilty of murder and sentenced to twenty-five and ten years respectively. Martin Pollard received an eight-year sentence for manslaughter. In court, Darren Stewart recounted how he had called police claiming he was worried about Steven who had been tormented and taken away by 'vicious strangers'. But under questioning they all soon confessed to having taken part in tormenting him, although they blamed one another for his actual death.

The judge at Truro Crown Court was damning in his summing-up of the couple whose relationship had been cemented by their mutual sadism and power-lust. 'Your victim was highly vulnerable,' he told them. 'He was subjected to sustained physical and mental attack, in which he was violently assaulted, degraded and humiliated.

'You literally bullied him to death!'

CHAPTER 10

# MR AND MRS MURDER

## FRED AND ROSE WEST

The man and the woman stand together in the dock. He is middle-aged and short with startling curly hair that adds extra weight to his already disproportionately large head. His features are strange, curiously unformed, like those of a child whose looks have yet to be defined. When he gives a nervous smile, his pale blue eyes are swallowed up in the soft, pasty pillow of his face. Even the gap between his two front teeth seems child-like – the kind of smile you see in a million gap-toothed school photos. The cheap suit he wears looks incongruous, like a small boy forced to dress up for a wedding he doesn't wish to attend.

The woman, on the other hand, is solid, heavy, and though a decade younger than the man, her bulky presence and drab, shapeless navy cardigan make her seem older than her years. Her pale, doughy face is dominated by huge purple-framed glasses, through which her large, dull brown eyes stare out impassively around the courtroom. Every now and then a pudgy hand goes up to smooth back her straight, mousy brown hair, cut unflatteringly just below the ears. The small mouth, a tiny slit in the wide, flat expanse of her face, is set hard as her gaze slides almost disinterestedly over the court officials. The one person she never looks at is the man sharing the dock with her.

As the proceedings draw to a close, the police officers flanking the man prepare to lead him away, but he resists and his blue eyes fix with desperate, silent appeal on the woman slightly in front of him. Tentatively, just like the over-grown child he resembles, he reaches a hand out towards her. Immediately the police officers step forward to push him away – but not before he has seen her reaction.

The woman in the dock has recoiled from his touch.

Six months later, the man is dead, his heart as broken as the lives of all the people he harmed. He has hung himself with a noose made up of strips of his bed-sheets attached to a ventilation grille above his prison cell door; he leaves behind a note for the woman: 'All I have is my life,' he tells her. 'I will give it to you, my darling. When you are ready, come to me. I will be waiting for you.'

To the outside world, Fred and Rose West were a travesty of humanity, a stain on the lives of all who came into contact with them, but in their eyes they were the two star players in the greatest love story ever told. This was to prove the most deadly delusion.

'Come on, let's do it again.' Rose's deft, questing hands, were already working their way expertly over his body, but Fred West was spent. Lying back on the unmade bed in the cramped, shabby caravan, he glanced over at the girl by his side. Lumpy, with the pallid complexion of a person whose diet relies more on sweets than fruit and vegetables, she wasn't the most attractive lover he'd had, but Rose Letts had something else, something worth more to Fred than looks or sparkling conversation. Just 15, she was only girl he'd ever met whose sexual appetite equalled, even surpassed, his own.

Rose's libido was so high that sometimes they even had to draft in other men to come to the caravan to satisfy her. The extra money these blokes paid to lie down in the narrow bunk came in handy, but she'd have done it for nothing – Rose was just like that.

Fred wasn't born yesterday. He knew the rumours about Rose – that she wasn't quite there and her own family called her 'Dozy Rosie' on account of the way she'd rock quietly to herself when she was alone; also, that her father was a violent bully who might even had slept with his own daughter, but none of that mattered to him. What Fred West liked more than anything else in the world, was sex. And in Rose, he'd met his match.

By this stage, in 1968, Fred was already 27, with two small children to look after – one of his own, the other the result of his wife Rena's affair with an Asian bus conductor – and a deep, dark secret. The year before he'd got into, what he called to himself 'a bit of bother': he'd entered into a relationship with a woman called Anna McFall, who'd acted as an unofficial nanny for his children after his prostitute wife Rena had gone back to her native Scotland.

Problems started when Rena was brought back to Gloucester in November 1966 to face petty theft charges and she and Fred got back together. Instead of quietly withdrawing from the scene, Anna became more and more possessive, wanting him to kick Rena out and commit to her. The final straw came when Anna got pregnant and began pushing to become the next Mrs West. She wrote letters to her family in Scotland, boasting about her wonderful new boyfriend and how happy they were together. Fred couldn't afford another baby, and he certainly didn't want to be married again. He panicked.

In July 1967, Anna McFall disappeared. It would be more than a quarter of a century later before the world heard any more about her – when her dismembered bones were dug up in Finger Post Field, just inside the Gloucestershire county border. The skeleton of her unborn baby was by her side. They were Fred West's first victims.

So this was the man the young Rose Letts fell in love with: a man living in a caravan with two small children he didn't know what to do with; a man many locals considered to have been irreversibly brain-damaged by a motorbike accident when he was just 17; a man of prodigious sexual appetite but little or no understanding of human relationships, a man who had already killed… who had realised two important things as a result. First, that sometimes the dead can just disappear without seeming to be missed, like a stone dropping soundlessly through the surface of the water, and second, that murder was exciting.

In November 1969, to the disapproval of her parents, Rose moved in with Fred. By this stage Rena had disappeared again and he was once more on his own with the two children – 6-year-old Charmaine and 5-year-old Anna Marie. Rose was put in charge of them, but at just 16 herself and emotionally immature, she was incapable of looking after anyone. Everything the little girls did annoyed her – why did they have to make so much noise? And did they have to be so messy?

Charmaine, in particular, wound her up. 'She's not even your own daughter,' Rose would complain to Fred. 'And yet you're supposed to look after her, feed her and put up with her moods. It's not right!'

At just 17, Rose gave birth to a baby of her own, a dark-haired child called Heather, and the family moved to a shabby rented flat in a draughty old house in Midland Road, Gloucester. Once there, the situation got even worse. Fred was sent to prison for a spell for theft and Rose, left on her own with three small children, found it impossible to cope. Increasingly she took her temper out on Charmaine, moving on from slapping her round the face to hitting her with kitchen implements or smashing crockery over her head. With her sexual playmate out of reach behind bars, devising punishments for Charmaine became one of Rose's secret pleasures. She'd tie the little girl's hands behind her back with a leather belt and beat her trembling legs with a wooden spoon or leave her tied to the bed, unattended, for hours. On one occasion the little girl was admitted to hospital with a bizarre wound on her left ankle that was never fully explained. Teachers who'd dismissed Rose Letts as unimaginative and dull would have been shocked at the inventiveness the girl displayed when it came to the chastisement of 8-year-old Charmaine.

'Darling, about Char,' Rose wrote in May 1971 in one of her frequent love letters to Fred. 'I think she likes to be handled rough. But darling, why do I have to be the one to do it?' Rose was just 17 at this point, but already she was showing signs of the woman she would become. A woman with so little empathy for the suffering of others that she thought 8-year-old girls enjoyed being brutalised, a woman with so great a level of self-pity that she considered herself to be the only victim in the increasingly sadistic punishments she doled out.

One day, just as with Anna McFall, little Charmaine went missing from home. When her sister Anna Marie came home from school and asked where she was, Rose told her that Rena, her mother, had come for her during the day. The same story was repeated to the girl's school and anyone else who bothered to ask, although in reality there were precious few who were interested enough.

But Charmaine was dead, a victim of one of Rose's rages that had spiralled out of control. Her corpse was hidden in the cellar. Fred didn't mind very much. His was a world in which children were plentiful and disposable, a world where people came and went and no one cared much either way. When he was released from prison a short while later, he and Rose took the child's body and buried it outside in the muddy yard near the back door. A builder by trade, neighbours were used to seeing Fred tinkering about with tools in the back yard, and he knew how and where to dig a hole without raising suspicion.

And so death becomes a glue that binds a couple together, murder an unremarkable fact of life, and other people just bit players to be manipulated at will, then cast aside. A twisted kind of love is cultivated from the rotten carcass of anger, bloodlust and contempt, and weeds grow over a forgotten child.

Now both Fred and Rose had killed, each of them learning three important lessons along the way: that murder was easier than you might think, that your mind cuts off from it allowing you to sleep at night, and that even while a body moulders in a dank basement, the world won't notice a thing.

Life at Midland Road became increasingly chaotic. Rose, who'd developed a taste for prostitution back in the caravan, entertained clients in one room of the house. Fred found it exciting to listen to the noises coming through the thin walls and he even installed spy holes so he could watch her 'at work'. He introduced Rose to bondage, to sex toys, to lesbian sex, to threesomes... and she took to it all, with a greed that surpassed even his own.

Little Anna Marie grew used to the comings and goings of strange men in the night, but she never accustomed herself to Rose's temper that could flare up in seconds, like a lit match on a petrol-soaked rag.

'Can't I come with you?' she'd beg her father if she saw him getting ready to leave, desperate not to be alone with her stepmother. But though Fred loved his daughter almost as much as he was capable of loving anyone, he'd never, ever take her side against his lover, his Rosie.

No wonder poor Anna Marie, trying hard to make herself invisible so as not to incur Rose's wrath, would dream of her real mother coming to find her, just as she had Charmaine. Maybe Fred would come with them and the four of them could be a proper family again like the other kids at school seemed to have, with mums who helped you with your homework and invited your friends round for tea, who didn't go mad if you dropped something or wet the bed or just happened to look at them in a way they didn't like.

Though her heart thumped expectantly at every knock at the door, Anna Marie was always disappointed. Her real mum would never turn up on the doorstep with arms open wide and Charmaine grinning by her side, but it wasn't that she didn't care. Rena West (née Costello) did indeed come from Scotland and was looking for her daughters in August 1971. She asked around in the village of Much Marcle, where Fred had grown up close, some said unnaturally so, to his mother Daisy. Now Daisy was dead, but her husband and another son still lived there and they told Fred that his estranged wife was looking for him.

'What'll I tell Rena?' Fred asked Rose anxiously. 'She's bound to ask all about Char.' Deep down, they both knew the answer to that one.

Some time in August 1971, Fred arranged to pick up Rena

and take her to see her daughters. Climbing into his car, she was full of anticipation for the emotional reunion ahead. But when the car eventually pulled up in front of Midland Road in the middle of the night, Rena didn't watch anxiously out of the window, patting her hair nervously and hoping to make a good impression on the daughters she'd travelled so far to see, nor did she leap out before the engine was even stilled, calling their names. Rena West was already dead.

More than two decades later, her body would be found buried in a field not far from Fred's childhood home. She'd been dismembered, limb sliced neatly from limb, head from neck.

Fred and Rose were married in January 1972 and shortly afterwards moved to a new home: 25 Cromwell Street, later known throughout the world as the House of Horrors. A tall, narrow and ramshackle house in a shabby inner city street peopled by students, transients and prostitutes, drug users and dole fraudsters, its long, narrow back garden was bordered on one side by the red brick wall of a Seventh Day Adventist Church, and on the other by a row of tall fir trees, whose long shadows cast the garden into almost permanent twilight. Once full of family homes, most of the houses in the street had now been converted into flats or bed-sits. They were temporary, uncared-for places, where people closed their curtains against the daylight and tried not to meet anyone's eye as they stood on their doorstep, fumbling with their keys. For more than twenty years, this would be home to the Wests.

To outsiders, the West family at number 25 were the epitome

of an ordinary working-class family. Dad was out at work most of the time and whenever he wasn't, he was often to be spotted making alterations and home improvements on the first property they'd ever owned. The children – and there seemed to be a new one born every year – were taken to school on time and collected every day by their mother, a plain, matronly-looking woman in tent-like dresses with little-girl socks.

True, there were a lot people coming in and out at strange hours, but that could be explained by the fact that the Wests took in lodgers in the upper rooms – the extra income helped pay off the mortgage on the house. Like many hard-working families, they appeared to be doing what they could to better themselves, and who could blame them?

In reality, the Wests were unlike any other family. Inside number 25, children were growing up in a house that was far from a home. Rose now had a special room where she entertained her male clients – equipped with sex aids, pornographic videos and, of course, a spy hole through which her husband could watch what went on. If she was bored, she might wander half-dressed up to the lodgers' rooms to have sex with one of the young men whose meagre rent helped to boost the family coffers.

Always quick tempered, now she rarely bothered to stem the rage that bubbled up inside her whenever the children were around. The kids - some of them Fred's, often fathered from among Rose's West Indian clients – quickly learned to do their chores and keep out of the way. Most of all they learned to keep quiet about the stream of young women who seemed to come through the door of the Cromwell Street house and leave suddenly, their belongings still scattered about for Rose to pick through. And they kept quiet about the screaming in the night and the beatings they endured – and quiet about the rape too.

Fred and Rose thought children needed to be 'broken in' to the world of sex by their parents. Your children, they believed, belonged to you just as surely as anything else. When Anna Marie was just 8 years old, her stepmother led her down to the soundproofed cellar in Cromwell Street. There, she found Fred waiting for her. On the floor were some cloths, a Pyrex bowl containing a vibrator and some tape.

'It's a dad's duty to help his daughter, so that when she gets married she can satisfy her husband,' Fred explained to the terrified child.

As Rose removed her stepdaughter's clothes, she echoed her husband's words: 'Aren't you a lucky girl to have parents who care enough to do this for you?'

Anna Marie was then brutally raped by both her parents, her cries unheeded in that cheerless cell. Later, they would make a fuss over her, rubbing kindness like salt into the very wounds they themselves had made, until the little girl didn't know whether to feel frightened or grateful, loved or abused.

This was Anna Marie's initiation into the nightmare world of Rose and Fred, but it was to be far from a one-off experience. In years to come she'd be raped numerous times, forced to join in group sex, held down while other visiting men assaulted her and made to work as a prostitute, just like her stepmother.

Over the years, others of the West children would also become all too familiar with that torture chamber in the cellar, where a child could be tied to a metal frame, her mouth stuffed with a gag, her screams dying in her own throat, knowing that no one would come to help her.

When it came to her turn, Heather, the eldest of Rose and Fred's natural children, refused to believe that what was happening in their house was normal. Instead, she fought back and resisted when Fred tried to 'break her in' and she got her sister Mae to stand guard while she showered. Rose was furious. 'She's a lesbian, definitely!' she sneered to Fred, eyeing up her 15-year-old daughter's defiant scowl.

In truth, Heather's rebellious stance masked her increasing desperation. She dreamed of leaving Cromwell Street behind, of living in a home where she wasn't beaten for being a few minutes late from school and didn't have to lie awake in the dark, terrified someone would enter her room uninvited or be forced to press her hands to her ears to block out the screams that echoed up the stairs.

One day, soon after her 16th birthday, Heather too disappeared, just as Charmaine had done, all those years before.

'Oh, she's gone,' Fred told the other children when they came home from school and asked about their sister.

'She got a job in a holiday camp in Devon. Someone came and picked her up in a mini.'

But there was no job and no mini – and there was no hopeful new future, no excited young girl waving from the car window. Instead, Heather had been strangled, either by Fred or

Rose, who were angered by her 'smirking', by her refusal to be moulded and treated as a possession to be used and re-used at will. Fred persuaded his oldest son, Stephen, to help dig the hole in the garden in which he buried his daughter, telling him that it was intended to be a fishpond. It would never have crossed his mind that something like that could permanently traumatise a boy.

Again, Fred dismembered the body before burial, chopping it into pieces and, as usual, keeping some bones back as a trophy. By this stage, he'd become quite an expert because Heather was far from the first victim to be buried in the soil of 25 Cromwell Street.

Over the years, a succession of young women had come to the house, but they never left. Some had come willingly, drawn in by the image the Wests projected of being a normal, loving couple.

'Come round for a girlie chat,' Rose would offer, her bland features arranged into an expression of sympathy. And so they would come: girls who were running away from care homes, girls in trouble with their parents, girls whose hard edges frayed away to nothing at the first sign of warmth and kindness, girls who wouldn't be missed when they were gone. Others were quite simply snatched off the streets by Fred and Rose, from late-night bus shelters or dimly lit corners where 'nice' girls shouldn't be after dark.

And what horrors awaited them in Fred and Rose's DIY dungeon? What abuses did they have to endure as slaves of a couple who, increasingly, were unable to separate sex from pain, gratification from humiliation? Some were kept just hours, others days... Some were made to wear masks, one with just space for a tube to be threaded into one nostril so that the girl could breathe. Some were suspended from a beam in the ceiling, others videotaped as they writhed in silent agony, with their mouths sealed shut by gags.

Two escaped. One, Caroline Owens, managed to flee after just one night. She tried to tell police what she had gone through, but in the end the Wests were accused only of assault and made to pay a derisory fine.

'I'll kill you and bury you under the paving stones of Gloucester!' Fred had threatened Caroline after raping her. She got the feeling that many girls were already there, forgotten women without names who'd vanished into a black hole on a seedy urban street.

The other girl, an underage teenager from a care home, couldn't bring herself to tell anyone what had happened to her, but instead wrapped her fear and trauma around her like a strait-jacket – damaging, restricting, suffocating.

Of course, the Wests made some mistakes. One of the girls they snatched off the street, Lucy Partington, was from a well-off, close-knit family, who scoured the countryside looking for her and made sure her photograph stayed in the newspapers, on the local news and pinned to lampposts. Lucy's uncle was the novelist Kingsley Amis, and her cousin was Martin Amis, also a novelist, who would later write about the effect Lucy's disappearance had on him in his autobiography *Experience.*

But with nothing to link Lucy to the Wests, and no clues as to what happened, the photos gradually faded, and headlines featured new mysteries, new disappearances. And somehow, in their squalid semi-detached, Fred and Rose continued to murder, and carried on raping their own children and burying bodies under their own cellar and back yard.

The end, when it arrived, came in the words of the TS Eliot poem, not with a bang, but a whimper. A 13-year-old girl who'd been assaulted by the Wests cracked and told a school-friend about the abuse. That friend went to the police. The policewoman assigned to the case, Hazel Savage, remembered the name Fred West from decades before when she'd come into contact with his then estranged wife, Rena Costello. She recalled the things Rena had told her about Fred's depraved sexual appetite and his violence.

Police arrived to search the house, taking away nearly 100 extremely hardcore pornographic videos, many of them homemade. Fred and Rose were arrested and the five youngest children taken into care.

'They don't have nothing on me,' Rose told everyone when she was released on bail on 27 February 1994. But slowly, the net was tightening on the West's house of hell. Hazel Savage went to interview Anna Marie, by now a mother herself and living on her own with her two daughters. From her she got the full story of a childhood lived in fear and in pain, of the parents who used her like a living sex toy and handed her round to their friends to share.

'Find Charmaine for me,' Anna Marie begged her, 'I've been looking for her for years.'

Interviewing Anna Marie's ex-husband who'd known the Wests well, Hazel Savage got a different message. 'Find Heather,' Chris Davies told the policewoman. 'She's who you should be looking for.'

But both Charmaine and Heather seemed to have disappeared into thin air, carried by the wind like the litter that blew along Cromwell Street. Gone, gone, gone.

Quizzed about what happened to Heather, Fred and Rose gave a succession of contradictory stories: she'd gone off to the holiday camp, she'd vanished while Rose was out shopping, she was making a fortune working as a prostitute and a drug dealer...

The Wests' sexual assault case collapsed on 7 June 1993 when the key witness, a 13-year-old girl who was never named, failed to turn up for the trial. Rose and Fred went home and their collection of pornographic videos, largely unwatched, was destroyed by the police. But while the couple celebrated, reassured once again that they were beyond the reach of the law, Hazel Savage couldn't bring herself to close the file. In her head she could hear Rena's voice echoing down the years. When she closed her eyes, she saw the young Anna Marie, betrayed and brutalised by the very people who were supposed to love her best.

Meanwhile reports were coming to her of things the young West children were saying while in Care. Social services were worried, in particular, by a long-running family joke among the children – that you didn't want to get on the wrong side of Fred or you'd end up under the patio, like Heather.

Could Fred and Rose really have had anything to do with the mysterious disappearance of their own daughter? The idea was unthinkable, unimaginable. Yet so much about the Wests appeared to be beyond a normal person's comprehension.

Hazel Savage began to press for a warrant to dig up the garden at 25 Cromwell Street. 'What if you're wrong?' she was asked, again and again. 'It's a lot of money to spend on some kind of children's sick joke.' But something told her she wasn't wrong. The bleakly paved strip of garden at the back of the Wests' house held dark secrets, Hazel was sure. Someone had to unearth them; someone had to stop Fred, with his creepy smile and roughened workman's hands... Someone had to stop Rose – with her little-girl socks and her collection of sex toys that looked like torture implements.

On Thursday, 24 February 1994, a police van pulled up outside 25 Cromwell Street. Rose was alone in the house with her son Stephen.

'What's going on? What are you doing?' she screeched, as police officers barged through to the back garden and started to pull up the paving stones while a mechanical digger manoeuvred into position. It was bitterly cold and the men's breath hung like mist in the dank air of the claustrophobic, narrow yard.

'You're going to make fools of yourselves,' Stephen told the police.

'That's up to us,' came the terse reply.

Rose was furious at the damage being done to her property. She played the affronted innocent householder to perfection. 'There's nothing you'll stop at, is there, hey?' Rose, with her big glasses magnifying her wide self-righteous eyes, her plump fingers jabbing angry holes in the air. Outraged, self-pitying.

When he returned, Fred accused the police of harassment. It wasn't fair. Why were they picking on him? Why couldn't he and his wife be left alone?

That the couple put on such a good show of being the injured party was not surprising. The Wests actually believed that what they'd been doing all these years – the rapes, the incest and the murders – was *their* business, just as their children were *their* possessions. No one else had the right to intervene.

But by the next day, with the noise of the digger ringing through the cheerless house, Fred realised the police were not going to pack up and go away. Sooner or later, they'd find Heather's remains – the question was, how many others would they discover in the process? He decided it was time to confess.

'I've done something really bad,' he told his son coyly. Standing at the back door of the house, he pointed out to police the spot where he'd buried Heather six years before.

'There's no need to dig anywhere else now, is there?' he told them.

But when police began to dig the unforgiving soil of 25 Cromwell Street, they came across bones belonging to two separate skeletons and they quickly realised that if Heather was indeed buried in the back garden of her own family home, she was not alone.

Fred now owned up to the killing of two more women, who were buried in the garden. Then, realising the search had spread to other areas of the house, he told police about other bodies buried under the cellar floor and the bathroom floor. He hadn't meant to murder anyone, he said, they were all situations that had got out of control. As for the rapes, well, they never happened. The women had been willing sex partners until something had gone too far. Rose, he insisted, had had nothing to do with any of the deaths.

After two weeks of searching, the remains of nine bodies had been found at 25 Cromwell Street, and the eyes of the world were fixed greedily on the tall, narrow house, where young girls' screams had gone unheard, and their bones had lain for years, decades even, largely unmissed and forgotten in the damp, dark earth.

But that wasn't the end. The bodies of Rena Costello and Anna McFall were soon discovered in the green rolling fields of rural Gloucester and the remains of little Charmaine unearthed from under the cellar of 25 Midland Road. A succession of yellowing bones, each one telling a different story, bearing witness to its own private horror…

Still Rose insisted she knew nothing, that she'd seen nothing of the young girls who came in the night and never left, of the bodies dismembered in the bath; that she'd heard nothing of the screams that rang out in the night, spoken nothing of the mysterious disappearances of her daughter and stepdaughter.

No one believed her.

Rose West was charged with ten counts of murder, Fred with twelve. The likelihood is there are many more bones buried, perhaps like Fred said, under the paving stones of Gloucester, many more victims unmarked and not mourned.

In prison awaiting trial, Rose turned on her husband. She was a victim too, she snivelled. That man had taken everything from her – her youth, her innocence, her daughter, and now her freedom.

Fred, who'd never shed a tear for his victims, now wept for himself and for the loss of a love that was, to his warped mind, pure and noble. He wrote letters full of longing and adoration to his 'Rosie' and sent messages of love via their children, who, despite everything, continued to visit.

But Rose never replied. In court appearances, she refused to look at her husband and shrank from his touch. Fred's heart crumbled to pieces until he could no longer see a way forward. He might, perhaps, have coped knowing that he would spend the rest of his life in prison. After all, he had his memories, sick and monstrous as they were. But he couldn't handle the loss of Rose. With her by his side, his basest thoughts had seemed normal, and with her encouragement, his desires had become realised, his fantasies made possible. Rose had been the fairground mirror in which his darkest, most twisted thoughts had been reflected back to him as somehow healthy. She had not only recognised the evil inside him, she had released it, welcomed it and made it part of their family life.

With her, he'd been the hero of his own love story. Without her, who was he? A grinning, puffed-up little man, whose depravities masked a deep-seated sexual inadequacy; a weak, cowardly man who exercised power only over those unable to stand up for themselves, who inflicted pain on those unable to fight back...

*'Happy New Year, darling... All my love forever and ever'*

Just minutes after writing these words to his beloved Rose on New Year's Day 1995, Fred West was hanging from a makeshift noose, taking his untold secrets of other burial grounds, other victims to his grave. Rose was on her own.

In October 1995, ten months after her husband's death, Rose West was found guilty of ten charges of murder after a trial in which the survivors, among them Caroline Owen and Anna Marie Davies, spoke for the dead with a dignity and a bravery that caught in the throat of all who were present. Yet Rose continued to deny any involvement, even in the face of mounting evidence of her cruelty, sadism and ungovernable temper.

Rose West is currently serving ten life sentences for murder and is unlikely ever to be released. She has never shown any interest in where her partner of more than half a century was cremated, nor what became of his ashes.

In the end, the story of Fred and Rose West is an inverted, macabre love story, starring the couple no one ever really looked at twice: the mousy, nondescript pair who got their kids to school on time and spent their money on home improvements. Ultimately, it wasn't guilt for the untold number of women he'd murdered that killed Fred, nor remorse for the killing of two of his own children, nor the sadistic abuse of their siblings; it wasn't an attack of conscience or the slow dawning realisation of the enormity of the crimes he'd committed... No, what robbed him of the will to live was the withdrawal of love. United, Fred and Rose had been responsible for some of the most depraved murders in criminal history. They had presided over a household of torture chambers and terror, where children's screams pierced the night air and young women lost both their innocence and their lives. Together they enjoyed family barbecues on the patio below which their own daughter lay buried and dismembered, her bones mingling with those of all the others for whom life had become such a living nightmare that death, when it came, was a welcome release.

Separated from the woman he loved, Fred West was nothing – a man-child left floundering in a world he could no longer recognise. Alone, he was still capable of murder and rape, but it was Rose who validated his urges, who made them seem normal, natural even, and who egged him on to ever more extreme displays of sadism and brutality, joining wholeheartedly in the torture, the sexual assaults, the killings...

...All in the name of love.

# BIBLIOGRAPHY

During my research into the particular dynamics of couples who kill, I was helped by numerous sources. The following books also provided valuable insight:

*All His Father's Sins: Inside the Gerald Gallego Sex-Slave Murders* by Lt Ray Biondi and Walt Hecox, Prima Lifestyles, 1991.

*Fred & Rose: The Full Story of Fred and Rose West and the Gloucester House of Horrors* by Howard Sounes, Little Brown, 1995.

*I Choose To Live* by Sabine Dardenne, Time Warner Books, 2006.

*Invisible Darkness: The Horrifying Case of Paul Bernardo and Karla Homolka* by Stephen Williams, McArthur and Company, 1999.

*Shared Madness* by Christopher Berry-Dee, John Blake, 2005.

*Son of a Grifter: The Twisted Tale of Sante and Kenny Kimes, the Most Notorious Con Artists in America* by Kent Walker with Mark Schone, William Morrow and Company, 2001.